To Karen
with
great affection —

DREAMSEEKER'S DAUGHTER

Carole A. Boger

The Goodlanders make Huck Finn look like The Man in the Grey Flannel Suit ~ New Orleans Times Picayune, 1957

"Borges' tale of her family's love, innocence, and courage invites us to learn the difference between dysfunction and creative cooperation. Their journey aboard the Elizabeth is a destination of the heart. Such an extraordinary and memorable trip!" ~ Vicki Hendricks, author of Miami Purity, Iguana Love, Voluntary Madness, Sky Blues, and Florida Gothic Stories.

This book is dedicated to my beloved grandchildren with the wish that they all dwell in safe harbors and honor their Dreamseeker genes: Caleb, Matt, Jack Borges, and Eli Goodman, Melissa & Josephine Peralta, and Danielle and Amanda Galbraith, and my great-granddaughter Cecilia Peralta.

Other books by Carole A. Borges:

Disciplining the Devil's Country
Published by Alice James Books, Farmington, ME

"Carole Borges' poems are risky in the best sense of the word: she is fully willing to see and be seen, to know and be known. Tender, headlong, angry, a genuine human presence emerges in these poems." ~ Mark Doty

"I like the mythic imagination present in these poems, the way the ordinary is rendered magical and portentous." ~ Claire Keyes

Book designed by Kim R. West

©2013 by Carole A. Borges

Knoxville, Tennessee

ISBN-13: 978-1478122579

ISBN-10: 1478122579

Contact Carole A. Borges at caroleann1@yahoo.com

Author's Note: The people, places and events in this memoir were recorded as faithfully as remembered. Some of the characters and a few of the businesses have been given fictitious names.

DREAMSEEKER'S
DAUGHTER

Carole Ann Borges

Acknowledgments

During the sometimes maddening process of writing this book the following people encouraged me and kept me sane. They cheered me on when my spirits sagged and bolstered me when my belief in myself waned. Special thanks to my wonderfully supportive family, especially my children, Gary, Angie, Cindy and Josh, my son-in-law David Galbraith, and my extended family of friends. I owe so much to the many cyber-friends I have met during the long process of completing this book. They have waited patiently for the day they could buy the book and lifted me up every time my spirits sagged. I would also like to thank Mark Doty and David Wojahn for the literary tools they added to whatever natural writing instinct I had and to Greenfield Community College, Salem State College, Vermont College's MFA in Writing Program, and the Knoxville Writers' Guild. Meg Bensey, my editor, deserves special recognition. I could never have completed this project without her.

Foreword

Memory is perhaps our most precious possession. It is uniquely ours, so I know my version of our life aboard the *Elizabeth* will conflict with my siblings' versions. That's okay. My brother Tim, a.k.a Capt. Fatty Goodlander, wrote a book awhile back called *Chasing the Horizon*. As I read it to Mom (she is legally blind now), she shook her head in amazement.

"Where does he get this stuff?" she asked.

"He makes me sound like a nymphomaniac," I groaned. But as we became enthralled with his story, we didn't care anymore. Reality is like Play-doh; it is soft and changes shape every time you touch it. I hope my version captures the essence of us. I hope it encourages people to pursue their dreams, because even though their dreams may not take them where they want to go, the riches they will accumulate along the way will be invaluable and amazing.

Whether it forms a lake, an ocean, or a river, water is a great teacher, and it can take you almost anywhere in the world. But first there must be the vision, the eye that opens onto a dream vista so compelling you can't resist its siren song. If you let the Dreamcrushers with their *shouldn'ts* and *don'ts* and *what ifs* discourage you, chances are you will never haul anchor to leave your comfort zone, but if you're a Dreamseeker, you will not flinch. In spite of all warnings, you will go.

The Elizabeth, St. Pete, Vinoy Basin

Chapter One

WHILE TRYING TO TEACH our class about percentages, Mrs. White, my fifth grade teacher, told us there were many different kinds of churches in the world. She said she was going to call out their names. When ours came up we were supposed to stand and go to that group—Catholic, Baptist, Methodist, Jewish. Each time she called out a name, a few kids would leap up, until eventually I was the only one left sitting.

1

"So what are you, Carole?"

I told her I was nothing.

"But you've got to be something, honey? What church do you go to?"

I told her I never went to church.

"Well, what were you baptized then?"

When I told her I wasn't baptized, she seemed very upset.

"But your parents must be something? What church did your parents go to when they were little?"

I told her my mother had been a Catholic, but she quit because a priest once told her if she married my heathen father her children would burn in Hell.

Groping for some justification, I finally blurted out, "I think it's my Dad's fault. He's part Indian."

Recoiling as if she'd discovered I had nits or something, Mrs. White wrung her hands. "Well I guess *that* means you're not even a Christian, Carole."

The embarrassment haunted me, so one day when I was at the library alone, I decided to try to find some answers. Fingering through the card catalogue looking for books on CHRISTIANS, I was about halfway through the stack of index cards when it jumped right out at me---*Why I Am Not a*

Christian by Bertrand Russell. Rushing to the shelves, I grabbed the book and read the whole thing in one afternoon. Apparently Bertrand Russell, a famous philosopher, had looked at all the dates in the Bible and discovered they didn't add up. He even questioned whether the Bible was truly the word of God like everyone thought. As I slid the book back on the shelf, relief flooded over me. For the first time, since the humiliation in Mrs. White's class, I felt happy. Suddenly being a nothing didn't seem like such a bad thing after all.

My father was a relentlessly happy man. His lanky six-foot frame could have belonged to a dancer, and he never stopped humming; like a bumble bee he stirred the air around him. Dad's long sensitive fingers held a paintbrush with authority. In 1939, the year he met my mother, his Goodlander Sign Co. signs dotted Chicago's south-side.

Mom, an Italian beauty with high cheekbones and big brown eyes, married him because he was the smartest, most worldly man she'd ever known. Mom wanted to live a glamorous life like the lives she saw every week at the movies, and she felt certain right from the start that James Edward Goodlander was her ticket out of the ordinary. Both my parents loved the movies, but I guess everyone did in those days. Once Mom told me,

"Growing up, I couldn't decide if I wanted to be a movie star or a gunman's moll."

Before I was old enough to play outside, there was only our third-floor apartment, a long string of rooms on Englewood Avenue on Chicago's south-side. Furnished lovingly by my parents, my bedroom sported a circus motif hand painted by Dad. One whole wall was a blackboard. In front of it, sat two little wooden desks with iron legs.

My father knew everything about celestial navigation, so on the ceiling, he painted all the major constellations with their names attached. At bedtime there was always a story, *The Wizard of Oz* or *Aesop's Fables*. Afterwards, we'd pile into my bed. Our bodies falling comfortably together, we'd gazed up at those stars as fondly as if they were real.

Because our windows were so high up, Dad could run around naked without worrying. Mom wasn't crazy about this idea, but Dad assured her there were people all over the world who never wore clothes. Mom kept telling him, "Put some clothes on, Edward," but it wasn't until the boys who lived on the third floor of the house across the street got a pair of binoculars that he relented. For several days they stood on the sidewalk beneath our apartment, yelling up at our windows, "Nature Boy! Nature Boy!"

I don't know how many times a week everyone else went to the movies, but we went at least once and often more. At the entrance to the Southtown Theater, swans swam in a black marble pool landscaped with ferns and palms, and I loved tossing copper pennies in to make wishes. The plots of movies back then were very simple. Good guys always won. Bad guys got shot. Virgins married handsome men. Bad girls got treated like dogs. But it was really the musicals that were our favorite. We'd go in and be dazzled by the mirth, elegance, and wit of Fred Astaire as he swirled Ginger Rogers across a white marble dance floor. Gene Kelly would tap dance along a rooftop with his arms looped around a couple of buddies; then they'd all take off dancing down the street. Coming home, Dad would do the same. He'd whistle and whirl and spin around a light pole or tap-dance around a fire hydrant. Sometimes Mom would say *Oh, Edward!* to my silly dad, as if she was embarrassed by his outrageous behavior, but we knew she loved it.

The soundtrack of any good movie has to express a variety of moods. I grew up on Carmen and Pagliacci, on Xaviar Cugat's lively tunes and Glen Miller's foxtrots. Sometimes Dad would grab Mom by the waist and twirl her so hard her skirt would spin up over her thighs. Other times, he'd give her the Rudolph Valentino tango, bending her so far backwards that at the end they'd both start laughing. Dad sang and played guitar and encouraged Mom to join in. The way their individual voices rose up, drifted off, and came back together in mid-air filled me with awe. They sang in two-part harmony and as soon as I could learn I joined them.

Mom was proud of the elegant apartment they'd rented. Rows of brass mailboxes with an ornate speaker system decorated the white-and-black ceramic tile foyer, and plush maroon carpeting covered the polished mahogany stairway. My cousin Mickey, who was three years older, lived in the apartment below us. As toddlers, the two of us spent most of our time hosting penny candy parties in front of the window that sat on the landing between our apartments--Mary Janes, Bull's-eyes, the tiny pastel sugar dots we called "pills." The inside door that led to the apartments was always locked, so visitors had to call us on the speaker to get buzzed in. At some point, Mickey and I discovered we could also talk between our apartments.

"Captain Video. Captain Video. This is Carole. Come in."

When Uncle Marty, Mom's brother, visited, Mickey and I shivered with excitement. Through the speaker in the wall, I'd hear my cousin's voice calling, "Come in, Carole. Come in. Old Money Bags is here." Uncle Marty was just a chef on the Santa Fe railroad, but he dressed like a millionaire, and he always gave Mickey and me money. His wife Frances, a platinum blonde in high heels, gave me a doll once, a fancy bride doll with a painted face and frilly skirt. "It's for your bed, honey."

Uncle Marty had wavy brown hair, gold rings, and shoes you could see your face in. "He likes to gamble," Mom explained, "and he's pretty good at it."

Uncle Marty always asked, "What do you kids want?"

"A cowgirl outfit with fringe on the bottom and guns."

"One of those yo-yos with a picture of your train on it."

Because we knew he was a successful gambler, Mickey and I started to invoke his name whenever we played games of chance. Mom taught us to play craps, so holding the red dice in our chubby hands we'd blow on them until they got hot. *Come on, Uncle Marty!* This was the ultimate weapon against any opponent.

On Fourth of July, Dad took us up to the pebbled roof where he'd shoot off his shotgun while we banged pots and pans.

When Halloween came, he insisted on taking me trick or treating. Usually we were bums. Flourishing a big pink flower that squirted water, he'd say, "Hey, check this out!" After blackening our faces with burned corks, we hit the streets running. Carrying our bags of loot, we'd head for the Chinese laundry where, giggling, we'd squat beneath its big plate glass window. The minute the Chinaman turned his back, Dad would pinch my arm and shout, *Now!* Popping up, holding tight to chunks of Ivory soap, we drew large, looping circles on the clear glass.

Most Americans in the Forties came from immigrant families. The Old World and old European ways were things to be discarded. My mother told me she felt horribly ashamed when her mother spoke Italian. *Ma, speak English when I bring friends home. This is America.*

My father's family had been in America so long that they didn't have that problem. His ancestry was a mystery lost in a blur of wheat fields and cows. When we were little and asked where his family had come from, he'd get very annoyed. "We're all Americans," he'd insist. "It doesn't matter whose father came from where."

Mom tried to gather what little information she could, but facts were hard to come by. Eventually our paternal great-grandmother admitted that her grandmother had been the daughter of a medicine chief from the Miami tribe. This important bit of history was only given with a promise not to spread it around. Apparently, the rest of Dad's family didn't want to own up to being Indians. Grandma said all Mom had to do was to look at Uncle Rollie to know it was true. In high school, my father's brother looked so oriental everyone called him *Chink*.

When Dad enlisted in World War II, he chose the Army Transport Service so he could be on a ship. I missed him a lot, but not as much as Mom did. Besides, I enjoyed getting the pretty postcards he sent from all the exotic ports he was visiting. Sometimes a strange-smelling package with colorful stamps would arrive. Inside, I'd find dolls, books, and whatever little trinket he thought his little girl might enjoy. Dad was a prolific writer, so he wrote long passionate love letters to Mom every day. She kept these in a small bundle tied together with pale blue ribbon in her cedar chest in the dining room. Years later, my sister and I would spend many delicious afternoons reading them, especially the ones about *The General* and *Miss Fuzzy*

Wuzzy. It took us awhile to get it, but at some point, we realized these were their pet names for their private parts.

When Dad was transferred to an Army base in New Orleans in 1944, Mom and I visited him for a week, just long enough to picnic in City Park and visit the French Quarter, just long enough for Mom to get pregnant. Nine months later, on September 3, 1945, the day Dad returned home from the war, Mom went into labor and my sister Gale Orion was born.

Some men came home from the war wounded; some made the ultimate sacrifice, dying on battlefields or blown to bits aboard ships. Our dad came home with a fever that raged through him like a wild malaria. He dreamed of buying a boat big enough for our family to live on, so he could take a long cruise.

"Let's buy a boat and sail way from here, Marie," Dad said. "I'm almost thirty. They've got it all backwards. Men work their whole lives hoping to get to retirement, but few of them make it. Every yachtsman dreams of a long cruise. I want to take go now while I'm still young. How about the South Sea islands?"

Neither of my parents had a happy childhood. Mom, the youngest of ten, suffered from shyness. Her Irish father often had to be yanked home by the cops, and he had a terrible temper. Mom longed for him to show her some affection, but the wounds of his poverty-ridden youth left him unable to reach toward anything but the bottle. Finally, when she was a teenager, he moved out. Mom felt relieved and told all her friends he was dead. But then one day, he ruined all that by walking past the schoolyard. *Hey, Marie! Isn't that your old man?* Mom burned with guilt for lying, but she had to keep it up, so she told them no; it was just someone who looked like her father.

My grandmother was the heartbreak in Dad's family. One day when my father was eight, she wrote a note saying she was going to the store for milk and never came back. My grandfather sank into a deep depression and ended up having to send the children to a Lutheran orphanage for a while. Eventually, he got them back, but my grandmother's abandonment left deep scars.

The sea had always surged back and forth through my father's life. When he was sixteen, he and his father built a small cat-boat in their back yard. Later, he bought a black-hulled sloop named the *Dorthea*, then our Friendship ketch. My first sea journey was a cruise across Lake Michigan, from Chicago to St. Joe. I was only three months old.

Mom wasn't much of a sailor, but she considered it a romantic hobby, and she liked being a member of the Burnham Park Yacht Club. She wore pert pedal-pushers with navy blue middy-blouses trimmed in gold braid, wide-brimmed straw hats for the sun, and bathing suits lavish with tropical flowers. Mom's love of fashion earned her a reputation for being stylish, and her willingness to spend every summer on the boat with Dad impressed all the men. At a time when most wives avoided coming down to the harbor or resented the time and money boats demanded, Mom was a dream wife, but the idea of sailing off to strange lands with two small children wasn't exactly what she had in mind.

"We'll see, Edward...we'll see...let's just wait awhile...."

"But I want to kiss life full on the lips now," Dad said. "Take this trip while I'm still young enough to enjoy it. Let's take the kids and get out of here now."

Mom wanted a house, so she bargained for time, but Dad's enthusiasm was infectious. Soon our parlor was littered with glossy sailing magazines showing families living aboard their boats. Piles of *National Geographic* with pictures of naked aborigines, green mountains, and tropical jungles leaned in stacks beside every chair. After supper, Dad unfurled colorful nautical charts across our dining room table. He held up pictures of palm trees and white beaches. "What do you girls think?" he asked.

"Wouldn't it be fun to live on a boat full time? Wouldn't it be fun to live like pirates?"

"Yeah! Yeah!" My sister and I chanted. "We want to be pirates! Please, Mom!"

The first day Gale started school, I was only eight. Dad was working and Mom wasn't feeling well, so I was supposed to enroll her. Holding my sister's hand, I taught her to look both ways before crossing the street. I walked into the principal's office and handed the secretary the envelope with the birth certificate Mom had given me.

 "My sister needs to register for kindergarten," I said.

Looking surprised, the secretary sized me up. "I'm sorry, but only an adult can register a child."

Gale, ready to shoot back home, tugged on my arm, but I stood my ground.

"My Dad said it would be okay."

"Well, rules are rules, dear." The woman shrugged. "You'll have to come back with a parent."

Not wanting to give up, I decided to try pity. Pulling Gale forward, I fluffed up her hair. "But she's been waiting so long. Just take her for the day. My mom or dad will come tomorrow."

The woman glanced at Gale sympathetically before picking up the telephone. "I'm really sorry," she said, "but, you'll have to excuse me."

As I herded my teary-eyed sister out of the office, I squeezed her hand. "Don't worry. Mom will bring you tomorrow."

Later, when I told Dad, he was proud of the way I hadn't just given up. "What do they need an adult for?" he said. "You're perfectly capable. What did they think? That you were trying to put something over on them? This is why I prefer being on the water. Life on shore is so complicated. All this red tape. All these rules. I'm telling you, Carole, we need to get a boat and escape all this nonsense."

On February 2, 1951, when our baby brother was born, Gale and I jumped up and down on Mom and Dad's big rollaway bed in the parlor. Finally, a boy! Now we were no longer just "the girls." When Mom asked what we should name him, I suggested Gary, because that was the name of my first real crush, a blond boy I met on one of my weekend journeys to the Museum of Science. Back then, the city was safe, so I could take the El by myself, and thanks to the generosity of Marshall Field, there was no admission charge at that fascinating place. Dad told me it was in the tycoon's will: children would always be free. I also enjoyed the Natural History Museum, the Art Institute, and the Lincoln Historical Society, where artifacts from the great president himself were entombed in glass cases.

"The girls are getting older, Edward. Before we know it, the baby will be walking. Shouldn't we look for a house?"

In the early 1950s, everyone was talking about Communism. Investigations began and newspaper headlines screamed *Red Under the Bed,* but Dad thought this was ridiculous.

"You know, I think buying a boat would be a better idea, Marie. This country is going nuts. I want to go someplace nice, someplace peaceful like the Islands."

Not being one hundred percent behind Dad's plan, Mom cranked up her campaign to get a house before Dad found a boat he could afford. Every weekend she dragged us through houses for sale, but Dad always managed to find something wrong with them--too big, too small, too expensive, or in the wrong location--but then one day Mom's dream house came along, a large bungalow with a wishing well in the yard.

"Couldn't we put a down payment on it, Edward?"

"Maybe we should wait...look at some more...see what's out there...."

Holding fast to his dream of a long ocean voyage, Dad spent every free minute he had trudging through the boatyards around Chicago. He also scanned newspaper ads, but nothing suitable could be found. Then one day a miracle happened. A few weeks before they were going to sign papers on Mom's dream house, Dad found the perfect boat. Coming home from work one day, driving along the banks of the Des Plaines River, he saw an old Alden schooner tied to a dock. She needed a lot of work, but the *Elizabeth* was beamy enough to live aboard, designed for long ocean passages, and she had graceful lines.

"Guess what?" Dad sidled up behind Mom to put his arms around her waist.

"What?" she said nervously.

"I found the perfect boat for our trip today! She's a fifty-foot Alden schooner built for long ocean passages. She needs a lot of work, but she is for sale."

After dinner, Dad called the owners, but they wanted too much money. He kept talking about all the work that needed to be done, but they countered by saying how famous she was, how she'd won the Mackinac Island Race twice and the Bermuda Race once. Her trophies were still on display at the Chicago Yacht Club. A classic boat like that would be worth a lot of money if she were restored.

For a few days Dad moped around. Even his vibrating lips fell silent. But then suddenly everything changed.

Bursting through the front door, he threw his coat down on a chair, grabbed Mom by the waist and lifted her off the floor. "You're never going to believe what happened! You know I've been stopping every now and then to see that boat. Well, today when I got to the dock where she was tied up, she was gone. I figured maybe they'd just moved her, but then I saw her. The boat sank, Marie! She sank! She's sitting on the bottom. "

"What?" Mom gasped. "She sank? Is that good, Edward? "

"Good? It's great!" Dad snorted. "They won't want much for her now, and raising her won't be that big a deal either. A deep-sea diver I know has been hounding me for months to paint his trucks. I'm sure I can barter something."

After Dad hung the phone up, he did a little jig across the floor. "I told you, Marie! Only five hundred dollars! The boat is ours!"

Mom's chin started to tremble.

"Aw, come on, honey." Dad pulled her against his chest. "You know how much I want this. In a few years, when we're tired of cruising, I'll buy you a house. I promise."

The first time I saw the *Elizabeth,* she was about to get hauled out of the water. It was a brilliant October day with a hint of coolness in the air. Rentner's Boatyard was a small enterprise perched on Chicago's southernmost edge. The boats stored there were lined up row after row along a set of iron tracks designed to carry a large lifting crane to the water's edge. Mounds of broken boards, loops of steel cable, and piles of long wooden masts set on sawhorses dotted the cluttered landscape. Tar was everywhere.

Holding Gary on one hip, Mom pulled us girls through the yard just in time to see the *Elizabeth* being shoved into a pair of heavy straps. Dad was racing around shouting orders to the men about to lift the boat, but the minute he saw us on the riverbank, he looked up and waved.

"This is a very important day for your father," Mom said.

I wanted to feel excited, but when they lifted the boat from the water, mud and green river-slime drooled out of every crack, hole, and crevice in the boat's stained and battered hull. It sluiced down her deck and oozed from her waterway. The man standing behind me laughed.

"What a lunatic! Can you imagine the work this guy will have to do?"

After the crane lowered the boat onto a cradle on shore, and all the gawkers and kibitzers drifted away, Dad came scrambling over to the spot where we stood. Flashing his Clark Gable smile, he threw his arms around Gale and me.

"So what do you think, kids? There's your new home."

"Hey, wait a minute," Mom said.

Dad laughed. "Well, it might be, Marie. You know in the islands...."

Gale and I had heard the same argument a hundred times. We knew who would win, so we set off to explore the boatyard.

White flight. The words have a soft sound to them, but there was nothing soft about the great migration that moved so many white people from the cities to suburbs. Overnight the complexion of Chicago's inner city neighborhoods changed, and ours was no exception.

It all started in Levittown, Long Island. Before the war, contractors on average built maybe three or four houses a year, but because of the new mass production practices he'd learned in the war, Mr. Levitt could build thirty-five homes a day. Even though later these houses would be made fun of---*and they're all made of ticky-tacky and they all look just the same*---to the returning veterans, they were castles.

Soon, spidery networks of suburban developments began to spring up on what was once Chicago farmland. At a time when it was impossible to find an empty apartment in the city, the suburbs were a godsend, and the financing was incredible. For only $100 down, a family could own a four-room house with a lawn out front and backyard for the kids. Most houses also came with a washing machine, an unheard of luxury in those days.

But the suburbs were only for white people. If you were black, no one would give you a mortgage, so that's what caused white flight. As most of our white neighbors moved from our middle-class neighborhood to the suburbs, the glut of available housing made prices drop. Suddenly black people, especially returning GIs, could afford to buy the empty houses in the city. Everyone said the blacks were trying to take over our neighborhoods, but it was clear the neighborhoods had really been abandoned.

It was a sad time for me as, one by one, the families I'd known all my life packed up and moved. When I heard Mickey's father was looking at houses in Michigan, it felt like my whole world was coming apart. My cousin was my best friend. I couldn't imagine life without him.

In 1953, when Mom finally agreed to move aboard the boat, Dad grabbed her hand and fingered her wedding ring. "Your mother understands this won't be easy," he said, "but she's willing to do it for me. I want you kids to know your mother is one of a kind."

Believing we'd soon be visiting other cultures, my father thought living with black people was great. Every time our door opened, he inhaled.

"Just smell those delicious smells! I wonder what they're cooking!"

He also liked the way black people talked. One night I found him listening to a conversation in the hallway.

Dat you, Bill?

Yeah, dat's me.

How you doin', baby?

Ah's tired, Momma. Ah's hungry. And Ah needs some lovin'.

Well, come on up, baby. What you need is sittin' pretty, right here on this couch.

Dad put his arm around me and chuckled.

"Don't they have a great way of saying things?"

21

In my sixth grade school picture, I'm the only white girl. Sitting front row center, with long straight hair and bangs, I'm wearing a plaid flannel shirt, Levis, and a thick black leather belt. I think the frown on my face tells it all.

No one enjoys being a minority. When my classmates ignored me or treated me like an outcast, it hurt. Sitting at my desk in school, I'd pretend to read when they passed around pictures of family vacations or shared gossip. When it came time for birthday parties, everyone in the class got invited except me. A few tough kids wanted to fight, but I wasn't the fighting kind. Eventually, I did make a friend. Her name was Serena, and I felt grateful for her friendship. Serena taught me how to play double-Dutch jump rope, how to rock back and forth until just the right moment to jump in. Serena called it "digging your potatoes." *Hey, girl! Git in! Stop diggin' them taters!"*

Two other girls, named LuWanda and Sheree, also decided to take me under their wing. They bragged that if someone gave me a hard time, they'd beat him or her up. LuWanda, a small, chubby kid with a face like a bulldog, scared me when I first met her. At school she was famous for getting in fights, but maybe because she felt sorry for me, she treated me like a little sister.

"Stop acting like such a scaredy-cat," she'd say. "If somebody's wantin' to mess with you, just hold yur chin high. Close your eyes, 'til they's just little slits. Then, shakin' your bootie like you was Mrs. Pahtootie, you just tell 'em to buzz off."

One summer night just before Mickey and his family moved to Michigan, my cousin wanted to take a walk. It was a hot summer night. The air was sultry, and the sky was already purple with the coming darkness.

Eventually, we ended up standing across the street from a red brick building with a group of black people in front. "It's a church," Mickey said. After everyone drifted inside, he steered me to the back of the building. Shoving a wooden crate beneath a window, he told me to climb up.

Inside the church, people were just settling down. Ladies with wide-brimmed hats perched like brightly feathered birds in the pews; mothers pulled their children onto their laps, and old men sat straight up on folding chairs. Finally, a skinny man with a tall pile of hair shooting up from his forehead walked to the pulpit. Behind him, three rows of blue-robed choir members swayed back and forth to music that sounded to me like roller-rink music. As it billowed throughout the hall, the man started speaking. "Will you be ready?" he shouted. "Will you be ready when Jesus comes calling at your house?"

As the man spoke, the crowd grew more excited. Some stirred in their seats, while others stood up. When he raised his black Bible over his bobbing head and started dancing, people started moaning.

"Jesus is our only salvation!" Spit flew from the man's lips. He patted his forehead with a white handkerchief. "Now ain't that what the Bible says?"

The crowd responded with a dozen yessirs and amens.

"And who loves Jesus?"

The man pointed his finger at the crowd.

"Do you love Jesus? If you love Jesus raise your hand!"

Suddenly, the whole congregation was on its feet, hands waving in the air. A multitude of bodies whirled into the aisles. When a man standing next to a tall freckle-faced woman started jerking and twitching around, she let out a loud scream.

"They're getting the Holy Ghost now." Mickey giggled.

Soon, the man began babbling. His eyes rolled back in his head and streams of spit flew off his lips. As the organ pumped faster, the choir shifted into high gear. They were all singing and clapping hands, and I swear to this day I could feel it too, the arrival of something so powerful it almost made me fall from my box. *Jesus! Yes, sir! Lord Jesus!*

A few months before we moved aboard the boat, Dad brought home a dog he'd swapped for a sign, a beautiful Irish Setter puppy with blue ribbons. He had a fancy American Kennel Club name --Jay's Gay Boy--but we just called him Jerry. I adored the dog and spent all my spare time taking him for walks or, because he was obedience-trained, putting him through his commands. When I mentioned that I might want to grow up to be a veterinarian, Dad, who was always happy to advance any ideas I might have about a future career, got all excited. He even made an appointment for me to interview a woman veterinarian. Every evening, for the next few weeks, he sat me down at the kitchen table to teach me how to conduct a successful interview. By the time we were done, I felt like a reporter for *Life* magazine.

On the day of the big event, notebook in hand, I walked the few blocks to 63rd and Halstead. As I strolled past the honky-tonk bars and the gypsy-parlors that dotted the busy street, I imagined myself a real veterinarian standing in front of a store with a sign Dad had painted in gold leaf--Carole Ann's Puppy Palace.

The minute I pushed open the heavy beveled-glass door of the Critters Wag Tails Animal Clinic, a pungent odor of urine and feces brought tears to my eyes. Pushing myself forward, I saw a bulky shape sitting behind a cluttered desk. After I announced who I was, a very large woman stood up. She wore a wrinkled tweed suit cut like a man's and a wilted bow tie. Because of her cropped hair, booming voice, and angular face, I wasn't even sure she was a woman.

Waving me into a chair, the scowling giant grabbed a stained coffee cup in one hand and leaned forward. "First off, it's not an easy job being a woman in this profession." One of her big paws pushed papers around the desk.

At that point, it took everything I had not to leap up and run, but I knew that would disappoint Dad, so I bent over my yellow tablet and started asking the questions. As I scribbled down her gruff answers, a chorus of yelps and howls kept billowing out of the back room--her unfortunate charges.

"You might as well know," she said. "Being a vet is no picnic. It's still a man's world out there. A lot of people don't trust a woman, so it takes a long time to build up a clientele."

After asking my last question, I thanked my potential role model for the interview and stood up.

"But wait!" She barked at me sternly. "You want to see the kennel, don't you?"

"No, that's okay." I smiled weakly. "I think I have all the information I need."

When I told Dad about it, he was working on one of his amateur radios. "Probably a lesbian," he said. "Some women want to be men. Some men want to be women, too. People make fun of them here in the States, but things like that don't matter in the South Seas. They're very broadminded there."

Our little brother had just learned to crawl when Mom suddenly announced she was going to rename him. "Gary sounds too much like Jerry," she explained. "Every time I say Gary, the dog's ears perk up, and he comes running. We can't change the dog's name. You can't teach old dogs new tricks, but the baby is little. He won't know."

I felt disappointed about this, but I thought the answer was simple. Mom was always calling our little brother "Teeny-Weinie." He seemed to like that, so why not call him Timmy? Timmy sounded like Teeny-Weinie. Mom thought my idea was perfect, so from that day on, Gary became Timmy.

Newlyweds enjoy a sail on Lake Michigan

Chapter Two

THE FIRST SUMMER WE lived on the boat, the novelty of it all kept us excited. Dad spent every free minute he had finishing her interior, while Mom doled out homemade lemonade and hefty sandwiches on paper plates decorated with colorful pennants and anchors. Gale and I wowed any visitors we had by reciting navigation rules we'd learned from *Chapman's Blue Book*.

When my sister and I weren't helping Mom with the baby, we wandered around the boatyard. A number of derelict hulks rested on the perimeter of the yard, sad reminders of dreams gone sour, but our vivid imaginations quickly turned them into pirate ships or yachts anchored in tropical lagoons. We were expert dumpster divers by then, with a passion for aluminum paint. Steering wheels, bulkheads, bunks, everything on our confiscated wrecks gleamed with a garish metallic glow.

"Ahoy there, Gale! Look smart! Pirates off the port bow!"

"We're in for a blow!" she'd yell. "Get those sails down!"

Dad loved seeing us play like this. Sometimes he even joined in the fun. Peering over the cap-rail of our ship, he'd shout. "Ahoy there! Permission to come aboard." Of course we always let him.

Hunched together, sitting on milk crates or gallon paint cans, we'd talk about our crew members, the good ones and the bad ones.

"Have you had any mutinies aboard this ship?"

"One." Gale pulled on her ear. "A real bad guy."

Spying a broken board lying on a bunk, I stuck my chest out.

"We made him walk the plank. Har. Har."

"Excellent move, Sir!" Dad patted me on the back. "Well, I see everything is under control here. Better get back to work."

When fall came, and we had to spend more time hunkered down inside the boat, our initial excitement waned. Our old apartment seemed spacious by comparison, and having the boat out of the water meant we had to climb a fifteen-foot ladder just to get to the deck. Dad had to carry the dog up, and water, and groceries. The galley sink wasn't connected, so Mom had a dishpan under it. When it was full, she'd send me on deck to throw the water into the river. This wasn't easy to do because, even though the *Elizabeth's* stern jutted out over the riverbank, it took quite a bit of force to not slosh it on the ground. Putting my foot on the very end of the stern cap-rail, I'd usually thrust myself forward, but one day the cap-rail gave way, and I went flying. I still don't know how I managed to do it, but during my 15 foot slow-motion fall, my hand instinctively reached out to a board fastened to the boat's cradle. For a minute I just hung there, my feet only inches from the ground.

Shaking, pulling myself back up the ladder, I remembered Dad had warned me not to step on that freshly glued board; so I knew he'd be mad. Sliding the companionway hatch back, my hands shook. I worried my knees might buckle.

"I fell off the stern."

"You what?" Dad looked up from the engine compartment. "You stepped on that board, didn't you?"

"I forgot!" I wailed.

Mom rushed forward to put her arms around me. "She could have hit her head and gotten killed, Edward."

"That's why it's important to obey orders on a boat." Dad threw his wrench down. "I hope, Carole, you learned your lesson. When I tell you not to do something, don't do it."

Sometimes when I was helping Dad work on the boat, I'd glance across the river to the street that led to the school we'd be attending.

"I hope the kids are nice there." Gale sighed.

"They will be," I assured her. "They're white, and we're white. I hope they have lots of parties."

Gale giggled. "You're boy crazy!"

Pinching her on the back of her arm, I squealed. "I am not!"

The idea of having friends thrilled me, so I kept imagining the fun things I would do once I had some. Maybe I'd even find a best friend, like the ones I read about in books, someone who knew all your secrets and wanted to be with you all the time.

The first day of school, the bus driver welcomed us with a big smile, but I felt shy. Trying my best not to appear nervous, I avoided looking toward the back of the bus. After shoving Gale into a seat up front, I shifted my eyes to the world outside the window--trees, neat suburban homes, station wagons in the driveways.

At first, I wasn't even sure the words were directed at me, but soon the chant that rocked the bus became undeniable. *Sunken Sailboat. Sunken Sailboat.*

As disappointment melted into embarrassment, I sank lower in my seat, but then the kid behind me started yanking my hair. Immediately, I thought of LuWanda, so I gave him my best bug-eyed stare.

"Screw off, Runt!"

"Ooooh! Ooooh!" The kid swiveled to face the rows of kids behind him. "I better be careful. Sunken Sailboat comes from the GHET-to."

As we dismounted the bus, I put my hand on Gale's shoulder. She was too young to know, but I did. With a sinking heart, I realized that with a family like ours and living on a boat, we'd never fit in anywhere on shore.

My new teacher, Miss Furlong, looked just like the Old Maid on the playing cards, frizzy red hair pulled back into a tight knot, a rosebud mouth below a sharp nose, and pupils black as

BBs. As wave after wave of pent-up emotion rippled through me, I noticed that her boobs were so long she'd incorporated them into her stomach and wrapped her belt around them. I couldn't help it. I giggled.

That was it. Miss Furlong stomped over to my desk. She grabbed me by the cheek and pulled hard. "I know your type. You're one of those tough city kids that think you know everything. Well, you won't be making any trouble in my class."

Trying to come to grips with the fact that a teacher had actually hurt me, I felt sick, and for the first time in my life, angry with my father. This was obviously all his fault, him and his stupid idea of sailing off to some place foreign. That's why I'd never have any friends. That's why we'd stayed so long in the old neighborhood.

After school, I slammed my books down on my bunk and stomped into the galley. Dad was sharpening a chisel. The sound of the blade scraping across his whetstone made me wince.

"What's the matter, honey?"

When I told him about the kids and Miss Furlong, he waved his hands in dismissal.

"What do they know? They're landlubbers, Carole! They have no imagination. They live in shoe-box houses, and they have shoe-box minds. Don't pay any attention to them. Soon we'll be sitting under palm trees in a place where everyone is always happy. They'll still be stuck here, freezing their butts off."

Dad always knew how to put things in perspective. In the Islands everybody loved one another. Of course, he was right. We'd fit right in there, so what did I care?

Chicago winters were cold. Our cabin heater used kerosene. It smelled oily, but when the north wind blew, we needed it to supplement the cast iron Shipmate coal stove in the galley. When we ran out of kerosene, I had to go to the gas station with Dad. Unfortunately, it was located next door to a busy hamburger joint where the cool kids from school hung out.

Battling the blustery winter wind, wearing knee-high rubber boots, a black watch cap, and heavy wool sweater, I'd see them inside laughing and dancing. Putting my head down, pulling my cap low, I would pick up the pace until even Dad's long legs had trouble keeping up. To ease my mind on those frigid walks, I'd try to calculate just how long it would be before we sailed into Paradise harbor. According to the plan, we'd motor down the Chicago River, then into the Illinois, then the Mississippi. In New Orleans we wouldn't have to worry about low bridges, so we could put up a mast and sail into the turquoise-blue waters of the Gulf of Mexico. Maybe we'd stay awhile in Miami or the Florida Keys; then we'd sail over to the Panama Canal. I'd read a lot about Tahiti, one of biggest islands in the Marquesas. Dad said it was a jewel resting among a long green chain of atolls. Wouldn't it be nice to live there?

Lucky for Mom, the *Elizabeth* had a large galley with a full-size red leatherette booth on one side. The bathroom or head, smaller than a closet, had a tiny inoperable sink, a musty hanging locker for clothes, and the shower Dad never did get hooked up. You had to pump the marine toilet by hand to flush it.

"Goddam hair pins!" Dad pulled clumps of rusty wire and matted hair from the skinny rubber hose that went into the seacock behind the toilet. He threw them into a bucket.

"I'd like to get my hands on the guy that invented those things. He ought to be strung up by the balls."

Dad seldom got angry, so it was impossible not to feel guilty, but without a shelf to set our toiletries on, what did he expect?

Mom and Dad slept in the main cabin in a bunk on the starboard side. A narrow wrap-around settee across from it acted as our living room couch. We did have a tiny TV, but we could only watch pre-approved programs. Lawrence Welk was okay, but not Alfred Hitchcock. Forward of that, Dad had a radio room where he could talk in Morse code to people all over the world. Gale and I slept in the fo'csle at the bow of the boat on a V-berth. Timmy slept curled on the cushions that surrounded the dinette table. The hanging locker Gale and I shared could only hold a couple of blouses, but we each had a narrow shelf above our bunk and a milk crate for special possessions. Above our heads, a big hatch offered us a patch of sky. In summer, fresh air flowed down. Sometimes at night, pale stars would appear, the kind Dad meant when he wrote "Stars: The Yachtsmen's Friend", an article about celestial navigation he sold to *Yachting* magazine.

In spite of Dad's promise to be in the boat yard only a year, the repairs were taking longer than expected. Two years later, the inside of the boat was somewhat shipshape and cozy, but there was still a lot to do on the hull. Dad, however, wasn't the least bit discouraged. He was living his dream and happy as a clam. Every night he took out his guitar and sang. He cracked jokes and chased Mom around the galley. He was always making a big deal about her breasts. "I took one look at those plump hound's ears," he'd say, "and that was it!"

Mom felt uptight about being so heavily endowed. "When I was a teenager, I used to tape them to my chest," she told me once. "I hated those things."

No matter how bad things got, Dad always managed to cajole our complaints away, and he never failed to remind us that all dreams demanded sacrifice.

Once I realized that we'd never fit in, never be accepted by regular society, I focused all my energy on helping Dad get us to Paradise as fast as possible. Every free minute I had, I worked alongside him, passing him tools, sharing his plans, helping him sand and paint hatches. Every night before I fell asleep, I imagined us sailing across the Pacific. Silver-blue porpoises swam around my pillow. *Wahines* in grass skirts danced at the end of my bunk, and the sound of beating drums echoed against the sides of the cabin.

By the time our third year in the boatyard rolled around, things were getting tense between Mom and Dad, and I was miserable. When Dad ran out of the money he got when he sold the sign shop, progress slowed, and to make matters worse, he decided Jerry had to go. After carrying the big Irish Setter up and down the ladder every day, he said it just wasn't worth it. Despite groans and moans from us kids, Dad found a man to take him. As I watched my beloved dog being led to the car that would take him away forever, I cried and cried.

Like every other 13-year-old girl, I soon became obsessed with the way I looked. To my surprise, some of the boys in my class had started flirting with me. Beauty, the great equalizer, made me realize that if I could only be pretty enough, no one would care that I was different or that I lived on a boat with parents who were drunk on impossible dreams.

Looking gorgeous, however, was a challenge. Not having a shower made me angry. Dad promised to hook it up as soon as the boat was in the water, but meanwhile having to take sponge baths in a plastic dish pan seemed downright depraved. One afternoon when I was being surly with Dad, Mom tried to make him understand that the conditions we were living under were hard for a teenager. Dad just shook his head and rolled his eyes. "Whatever you do, Carole," he said, "don't grow up to be a woman." He said it like he was just joking, but I didn't think it was funny, and years later, my shrink would call it "damaging."

Balancing glossy movie magazines on the dry rim of our tiny, inoperable sink, I spent hours trying to copy Bridget Bardot's pout. Pulling my long hair into double ponytails, I lavished my lips with pink lipstick. Peering into the tiny round mirror in the dimly-lighted head, I tried to perfect a French accent. *Ooo la la!* I thought I looked utterly fabulous, but Dad didn't appreciate my blossoming beauty.

"It looks like a bee stung you on the mouth."

During the 1950s, skin-tight Levis and crisp blouses, unbuttoned as far down as possible, were all the rage. When Dad realized I was purposely exposing my skimpy cleavage, he went ballistic. He found short-shorts especially lewd, and he hated flats.

"Sure, shoemakers love those things," he ranted. "How much do you think it costs to make them? The less leather they use, the more they charge."

One night he waved a mail-order catalog for nuns' shoes under my nose. "Just look at how strong these shoes are, and they're very attractive too. Now that's what I call a sensible shoe."

Rushing to my defense, Mom waved a handful of clipped magazine articles in Dad's face. "It's her hormones. It's just a stage, Edward. I'm sure she'll grow out of it."

After I graduated from elementary school, things definitely got better. There were only two groups of kids in my high school---the Collegiates---the good-kids, or the Hoods or

Hoodlums---the bad kids. The good kids obeyed their parents, got high marks in school, and entertained themselves with parties in their homes. The bad kids crawled through the streets, wore clothes that got them expelled, listened to nobody, and were mostly focused on sex. Considering it was the good kids that shunned me, the ones who still called me Sunken Sailboat or Tugboat Annie, you can guess which group interested me the most.

One hot July night, behind the elementary school, I let Paul Stevens feel me up. "Just pretend I'm Livingston," he said, "and you're Africa." As he proceeded to map all the mounds and plains of my body, he let out a soft moan. "Oh, these must be the mountains."

Dad knew something was brewing, so he started following me around, trying to catch me kissing boys or smoking cigarettes.

"Maybe, Edward," Mom suggested, "Carole is at a stage where living on the boat is too hard for her. Maybe we could keep the boat, but get an apartment too. At least until she is out of high school."

Dad rubbed his thumb across his cheekbone. "Move off the boat?" Dad gasped, like she was suggesting we migrate to the moon. "You're talking mutiny there, Marie. I promise I'll have the boat done by summer. Once we're on our way, she'll come around."

The winter of 1956 was brutal. The icy winds that whipped through the boatyard challenged both our heaters. Because of a huge amount of dry rot, Dad had to remove almost six feet of planking in the hull. He'd covered the big hole with a black tarp, but the thick flap of canvas barely kept the cold out. One December night, we were all sitting around the dinette booth eating supper, when Mom let out a scream. "Oh, my God!"

When she saw the man's head pop up right next to her feet, Mom leaped backward. To our astonishment, the head swiveled around a few seconds, and then it withdrew. A few minutes later, we heard footsteps crunching around in the snow, and a man's voice reporting. "There are people in there! They're *eating!*"

When I saw the color drain from Mom's face, I thought she might announce right then and there that she was jumping ship. Like in one of those corny dioramas in the Museum of Science and Industry, I felt my family frozen in time. I could almost hear some museum guide announcing, "Now here, folks, we have a Goodlander family. They are sitting down to dinner. The Goodlanders lived in boats. They are shown here on the Calumet

River. Though their living conditions were sometimes hard, they were a very interesting tribe. Meat loaf was one of their staples."

Our fourth and final year in the boatyard was the worst. Dad worked day and night trying to get ready for the big launch. Gale was bored. Timmy, a toddler now, was driving Mom crazy in such a small space, and I, having finally become popular with at least some of the kids at school, suddenly decided I didn't want live on the boat anymore.

"But I've finally found friends," I whined. "I hate living on the boat. Can't we just get a house and stay here?"

Because Mom considered my new friends hoodlums, for once, she sided with Dad.

"Oh, Carole," she said. "Look how hard Dad has worked. I thought you were all excited about our trip? Once we're underway, you'll change your mind. You can make friends anywhere."

"Those kids aren't really your friends," Dad said. "They're punks. By the time we get to St. Louis, they won't even remember your name."

At one point, one of the nicest kids I knew, a red-haired boy with a crush on me, said if we got married my parents wouldn't be able to drag me away. Even 13-year-old kids could marry in the south, and I was already fourteen. His brother had an Oldsmobile. We could be in Mississippi in no time. "Come on, let's do it!"

I was flattered that he cared that much about me, but I knew that would never work. He hadn't even finished high school, so how he was he going to support me? Besides, I couldn't hurt Dad like that. Angry and confused, I started acting out. I smoked more and got into heavy necking. One day I even shoplifted a fake ponytail from Woolworth's. *So what!* One of the benefits of being a sea gypsy, I realized, was having a clean slate in every town.

My biggest problem that summer was maintaining my role as a bad ass. It wasn't who I really was, but if I wanted to stay popular with the crowd I was hanging with it, it did seem necessary. Sometimes their behavior scared me. The boys kept getting in fights, and it wasn't just pretend fighting, either. A few kids got arrested, but only for drag racing or being drunk. The girls mostly talked about sex. Gathering together in the bathroom of the Dalton movie theater, they talked about Sandra Clark, how she had already done it. The hard thing the boys had in their pants. The way, when they pressed it against you, you got hot and dizzy. Wanted only one thing.

A short time before we left Chicago, I met Rex Thornton, a cool motorcycle guy with a fuzzy red beard and curly red hair. He was older. He could have been thirty, for all I knew, but I didn't care. I loved roaring down Chicago's sultry streets, him leaning low over the handlebars, me with my arms tight around his waist. When I buried my nose in his leather jacket, it smelled sweet, like trouble.

I'd always made sure to meet Rex far away from the boat, but one day, when I didn't show up, he came looking for me. When Pug Rentner, the yard owner, spied him and five other Harleys wheeling into the boatyard, he called the cops. Thank goodness, my parents had gone shopping. After I explained they were friends of mine, Mr. Rentner sent the police away, but he grabbed Rex by the arm.

"What the hell are you doing? Haven't you ever heard the word jail-bait?"

When Rex heard how young I was, he and the others left in a roar of dust.

"Please, don't tell my father about this," I begged. "He'll kill me."

Even though Pug Rentner thought our parents were crazy, he felt sorry for us kids. Gale and I had a big crush on him. We flirted with him all the time, and we knew he liked it. After a lot of pleading, Mr. Rentner finally relented.

"Oh, all right. I won't say anything, but I'll sure be glad when you people get out of here."

Because of the Rex episode, I decided it might be wise to take a step backward from my life of excess and crime, so once again, I started staying home to help Dad.

Dwarfed by the rising curve of the *Elizabeth's* hull, we were sitting on milk crates, polishing the brass portlights he was ready to install. "All I have to do," he said, passing me a rag wet with Brasso, "is paint the hull and get the engine running, and we'll be on our way. I know this hasn't been easy for you, Carole, but you'll see. It's whole different world in the tropics. We'll be spending time with people more like us. I can hardly wait to leave this grimy city behind."

Every time Dad talked about the wonderful life we'd have once we got sailing, my heart melted. I loved him so much. We all did. So what if we had to make sacrifices to make his dream come true? It was our dream, too, wasn't it? Handing Dad the portlight I'd just polished, I swallowed hard.

A couple of weeks after vowing to stay home more, I happened to meet a new friend. Her named was Colleen O'Connor. She lived at the end of the block by the boatyard, so every time I went to the store, I'd see her sitting on her front porch. One day she waved at me, and I waved back, then pretty soon we were talking. Colleen seemed like a nice quiet girl. She said she was going to become a nun. The only problem was, she didn't want to be one. Apparently, her mother had once been so sick the doctors thought she might die. Looking for a miracle, Mrs. O'Conner made a vow: if God let her get better, any daughter she had would be given to the Church. Colleen loved God. She was always talking about religion. But having to live in a convent, to never be able to have a normal life? Because of all the stress, Colleen turned to alcohol, Jim Beam whiskey, to be exact. One night, when her parents went out, she raided her father's liquor cabinet, and we both started drinking. Things were going along pretty well, until my stomach started gyrating. Hugging the toilet, I was sure I was going to die, but Colleen just stood leaning against the door frame laughing. As soon as I could get my bearings, I headed home, but on the way, I slipped on some ice and fell into a snow bank. Flailing my arms around, I tried to get up, but my body felt heavy, and everything was spinning around. For a long time I just lay there praying, *Please, God, if there is a God, I'm sorry. I want to be a good girl. I just don't know how.*

After that disaster, I sank into a fog of self-loathing. Obviously when it came to choosing friends, I was the dumbest kid on earth. I was beginning to doubt if I'd ever have a real friend when Donna Mancotti walked into my high school English class. She wore a turquoise cotton skirt that ended at her ankles, silver cowboy boots, and a brown cowboy hat with a red feather. Her strawberry blonde hair was done up in banana curls that fell to her waist, and she had the sweetest smile I'd ever seen. Realizing the other kids would laugh at her weird clothing, and remembering how hard it had been for me when I was the new girl, I sought her out as soon as the lunch bell rang.

As it turned out, the two of us had a lot in common. First of all, she didn't live in a house; she lived in an Airstream trailer in a trailer park across the river from the boatyard. The Mancottis were a missionary family who had just come from a Navajo Indian reservation in Arizona where they were trying to save drunken Indians. Mrs. Mancotti, a short, fat, moon-faced woman with stringy black hair, said the Lord told them to go to Arizona. None of them spoke Navajo, but the minute they stepped onto the reservation, a miracle happened: just like that, they could talk and understand the language.

Donna's trailer was so long and narrow it could have been a boat, and the Mancottis were even stricter than Dad. Donna couldn't smoke, dance, or even go to the movies. She had to go everywhere with her parents, and the only place they ever went was to prayer meetings in other people's houses. When Donna told me she sang and played guitar at the prayer meetings, I was dazzled.

Before long I was spending all my spare time with the Mancotti family. My new friend taught me to sing gospel songs. Eventually her mother sewed matching outfits for us--long, white cotton skirts with tiny little rosebuds and frilly white blouses. When we stood together in front the mirror, we looked almost like twins, and to me that was heaven. To my delight, I discovered I loved performing. I especially loved the way my voice vibrated when I sang, "*In that City. Holy White City. I have a mansion, a harp and a crown...*"

In spite of his aversion to organized religions, Dad was glad I'd finally found a friend who met with his approval. He said he appreciated the Mancotti family's closeness and the fact that they were moral people.

One warm summer evening, when Donna's parents had to rush across town to console someone having suicidal thoughts, a funny thing happened.

Donna asked. "Want to see something interesting?"

"Sure," I answered.

"Then follow me."

When we got to her parent's bedroom, she gestured toward the bed.

"Just sit down there."

After rummaging through the bureau opposite me, she came over to drop a flesh-colored thing that looked like a rubber pancake into my lap.

"It's a diaphragm," she said. "My mother sticks this in her pussy so she won't get pregnant."

Trying not to notice the way she was flopping the repulsive object around, I felt confused. *Had holier-than-thou Donna really said pussy?* I was hoping she hadn't, but there she was, rubbing the flesh colored circle against her cheek like a kitten with a catnip mouse. After a few minutes, Donna sat down next to me on the bed. As she slid her hand under my skirt, her eyelids dropped slowly over her big blue eyes. "I want to do what a guy would do," she said, pushing my legs apart. "You're my best friend, Carole. I love you." Then she kissed me, and, in a swoon, I kissed her back. In the end, we both got so carried away we almost didn't hear the truck door slam.

"Oh, my God, They're back!"

After Mr. and Mrs. Mancotti wheezed in with the groceries, Donna and I started putting stuff away. I was still a little dazed, but the act of stacking canned goods in the cupboard calmed me. Del Monte green beans...Hormel chili...Spam....

After the groceries were put away, Mrs. Mancotti put her arm around my waist, but I could barely look at her. "We're having a special healing group here next Wednesday," she said. "I hope you can come, Carole."

Peering over Mrs. Mancotti's head, I saw Donna sitting primly on the couch with her legs crossed at the ankles, an open Bible in her lap.

Knocking on the silver door of the trailer the next Wednesday, I felt excited. From all the cars and trucks parked around the trailer, I could tell it would be a good meeting.

Donna was sitting on the couch with two old ladies and a man in bib overalls, but she scrunched right over to make room for me.

After a few minutes, Mrs. Mancotti called the meeting to order. "Okay, folks," she said. "The Lord has asked us to call this meeting. He said there are sinners among us who need to repent. Suffering sinners whose only hope is to be washed in the blood of the Lamb."

The woman next to me pulled her Bible to her chest.

I seldom listened to what was said during the prayer meetings; all I cared about was being with Donna, but that night the energy in the room felt electric.

"Tonight," Mrs. Mancotti said, "we will begin our meeting with a few songs."

Donna and I started slowly with *The Old Rugged Cross,* but by the end we really had them rocking. Hands clapped, boots stomped, and the applause was boisterous.

After we sat down, Mr. Mancotti read a few passages from the Bible. Then he asked everyone to pray with him.

"Lord, we ask that you to be with us tonight. Thank you for the promise of eternal life. Tonight, Lord, we ask you to heal any heart blackened by Satan's stain, to let your Divine Light cast away any shadows. We ask this in your Holy Name, and in the name of your son, Jesus Christ."

At that point, Mrs. Mancotti put her hand on my shoulder. "Carole," she said, "Do you want to accept Jesus into your life tonight? Do you want to be saved from eternal damnation and live in the house of the Lord forever? If you do, stand up."

Shocked that she was singling me out, I moved closer to Donna, but my friend pushed me forward. "Go ahead," she said. "They're just going to pray over you."

I didn't know what else to do, so I stood up.

"Praise, Jesus!" Mrs. Mancotti shouted.

As she drew closer, I realized Mrs. Mancotti was sweating. Her pock-marked nose and yellow teeth were only inches from my face. Pinto-bean breath blasted into my nostrils.

Pushing me to my knees, Donna's mother straddled my body. When she shoved my head down, all I could see was ankles and shoes. I wanted to get back up, but scores of hands pressed me toward the floor. The smell of their kerosene heater made me nauseated. Sweat ran down my cheeks. All of a sudden, the reality of what was happening became apparent. They were going to ask me if I wanted Jesus Christ to be my personal savior, but I wasn't ready for that. All I wanted to do was run, so pushing Mancotti off my back, I sprinted toward the door. Panting like a dog, I flew out of the trailer park, ran over the bridge, and scurried back to the boat.

When spring came Dad told Pug Rentner we'd be putting the *Elizabeth* back in the water on the first of October. Mom's spirits soared, but I still had doubts. One day I'd feel happy that we were finally going to start our trip down the river, but the next I'd be mad at Dad for wanting to escape a normal life. Like a tightrope walker, I tried to achieve balance, but every time I did, someone or something knocked me down. In spite of this, I was doing okay, until my gym teacher handed me that note that said from then on we all had to wear green one-piece uniforms. The note stated how much the mandatory outfit would cost and when to bring the money.

I didn't like the gym teacher. Her booming voice and fat belly stuffed into too-tight, baby-blue sweatpants weren't her worst attributes. Miss Lowenstein (everyone just called her Miss L) also had hard eyes, like pig's eyes or crocodile eyes.

"Here's a note from school," I told Dad. "I need to bring the money tomorrow."

Today parents pay for school supplies, but back then no one had to pay for anything. Pencils, crayons, notebooks, everything was provided by the public school system, so when Dad read the note he was shocked.

"Four dollars? That's crazy! They can't *make* you buy anything, Carole. Just wear your shorts and a t-shirt."

The next day when I came into the gym, I pulled Miss L aside. Speaking as softly as I could, so the other kids wouldn't hear, I told her my father said the school couldn't make us buy anything.

"Well, you tell him, we certainly can!" she said loudly. "No gym suit, no class. No class, no grade. If he wants you to fail, that's fine, but until you have the proper attire, you can't participate."

As Miss L moved closer, I took a step backward, but she kept advancing. Her head swayed back and forth like a bull about to charge.

"Doesn't your father care about your education? He's the only one who has refused." Her balled-up fists thumped against her hips. "You go sit on the bench."

I hated sitting alone in the bleachers while everyone else took the class. The longer I sat there, the more I hated Miss L. Why did she have to make a big scene? Why did she have to say that in front of all the other kids?

Returning home, I dreaded having to face Dad. "They do have the right to ask you to pay for the gym suit," I said. "Miss L said so. All the other parents have already paid. Today she made me sit on the bleachers during class." I was hoping my voice sounded matter-of-fact, but the words were barely out of my mouth when I saw Dad's jaw start to twitch.

"This woman sounds like a nut. She doesn't know what she's talking about. You tell her I said you don't need a gym suit to take gym class."

"Yes, I do."

"No, you don't."

"Yes, I do."

Back and forth, I skated between them, and my frustration grew with each turn.

"I don't care what your father says!" Miss L shouted on that final, fateful day. Her face was so close to mine, the freckles on her neck folds seemed magnified. As her stiff pointer-finger edged toward my nose, I felt dizzy. *Please don't!* I begged, but she didn't stop. When her finger got too close to my trembling bottom-lip, my mouth opened. I didn't bite down hard. I just held the finger lightly, but all hell broke loose.

Accompanied by Miss L and the school policeman, they shuffled me off to the principal's office where I was immediately expelled. *Ha!* I thought. *No more school? Who cares!* We'd be leaving Chicago that fall anyway. Summer vacation was only a few weeks away. If I left home every day when I was supposed to, my parents would never know. I was too old to skip down the sidewalk, but that's how I felt.

In October, 1957, the *Elizabeth* was finally put back in the water, and a small crowd of people gathered. Some were friends. Others were just curious. Many still thought Dad was crazy.

Once, when I asked him why some people thought the idea of taking such a great trip was goofy, he told me it was because some people hated anyone who dared to dream big.

"There are only two kinds of people in this world, Carole. Dreamseekers and Dreamcrushers. The Dreamseekers relish everything that is life-enhancing. They promote exploration and daring. They see visions and act on them. The Dreamcrushers are the ones who always say you can't, you shouldn't, or that's stupid or crazy. Dreamcrushers are everywhere, especially living on land, and they come in a variety of disguises, too. They can seem nice as pie until you tell them some dream you have, and the next thing you know, they're putting you down, trying to make you as stuck as they are. Whatever you do, Carole, don't let the Dreamcrushers get you. Follow your heart. Chase rainbows. You'll be much happier if you do that."

On the day of our launch, the yard crew attached a cable to the *Elizabeth's* cradle and winched her to an open area in the middle of the yard. Pug Rentner slipped a pair of heavy steel slings under her keel and gave a nod to the crane operator. The *Elizabeth* hung suspended for a moment in mid-air, then she was lowered into the water

Hip! Hip! Hooray! Once the boat was baptized again, a loud cheer went up

The first time I stepped aboard the boat in the water, it felt strange. For so long the *Elizabeth* had been accessible only by ladder, but now I felt her buoyancy. Gently surging backward and forward with the current, it was almost as if she knew what grand adventures lay ahead of her, and I felt a renewed interest in our trip. Soon we'd be swimming in warm waters, eating bananas right off the trees.

The next few weeks slid past in a whirl of preparations. While Mom busied herself below stowing things, Dad and I got a feel for the boat. Several times a day, we'd take her out into the river and return to the dock. I'd been aboard boats my whole life, so I already knew when to jump ashore and how to tie the boat's lines securely, but after so long on dry land, it felt a little awkward.

The night before we left, Mom and Dad were sitting on deck surveying the freshly painted cabins, the varnished hatches, and the new stainless-steel lifelines. It could have been the Queen Mary they were admiring. Kneeling right behind them, practicing how to roll the stern-line into a flat "pancake" coil, I heard Mom say, "She really looks ship-shape and beautiful, Edward. You've done a great job."

Dad leaned his head against Mom's shoulder. "I couldn't have done it without you, Marie."

Seeing them like that, my heart melted. *Didn't I have the best parents in the world?*

The day of our departure dawned bright and sunny. After Mom rustled up a hearty breakfast on the Shipmate stove, we all hurried on deck to watch Dad untie the *Elizabeth's* dock lines. As she slipped quietly into the current, I walked forward to the bowsprit. It was six feet long and a foot wide, so I could stand at the end of it holding onto the forestay or sit with my feet dangling above the water. As the *Elizabeth* moved into the current and headed downstream, Rentner's Boatyard fell astern. It looked smaller and smaller. Then there was a bend in the river, and that part of our lives disappeared forever.

Gale, already an Indian expert at ten.

Chapter Three

WE SPENT OUR FIRST night downtown under the arched span of the Michigan Avenue Bridge. Dwarfed by the tall buildings around us, our boat and our lives seemed very small. That night when Dad took his guitar out, we all joined him in singing, our voices echoing out over the Chicago River, rising up against the city skyline. The white Wrigley Building with its huge spotlights loomed overhead like a giant ghost. We knew the hive of the city above us buzzed and roared with noise, but down there everything was private, and we were thrilled to be celebrating a great moment in our lives.

Anxious to finally be on our way, we were eager the next morning for the *Elizabeth* to join the line of boats steaming downriver. Barges carrying soybeans, wheat, steel or coal thumped importantly alongside her, and every time another boat came toward us, it tooted its horn. One whistle meant I'm altering my course to the right. Two whistles meant left. Huge cargo ships and oil tankers steamed past us, and small pleasure craft and fishermen in skiffs hugged the shore to get out of the current. They always waved, and we waved back because now we were river folk too, part of a larger family.

As the days passed, we settled into a routine. Mom fed us breakfast while Dad dialed his radios to listen to the captains on the other boats exchange gossip or news about the river downstream. Gale, Tim, and I washed and got dressed while Mom cleaned up, and then we all went on deck. Because we were mesmerized by the novelty of parading boats and passing shoreline, we usually stayed there all morning. I loved to draw, so I spent most afternoons sitting on my bunk with my back against the hull drawing pictures. Mom thought I had a real talent for art. "All your faces have personality," she said. "I sure wish I could draw."

Keeping Timmy busy was a challenge. Like all six year olds, he wanted to be the center of attention. For a while he was crazy about those little green Army men. He'd line them up and wage intense battles on the dinette table, but when he started talking to them like they were real, Mom banished them. "Imagination is one thing," she said, "but he's named them all. You and Gale need to play with him more." So Gale and I obliged her by playing endless games of War with our fidgety brother. Tim loved playing cards, especially when he got an ace. Slamming his prize down, he'd scream *War!* and Gale and I would groan like we were mortally wounded. Gale was studying Indians, so she usually read in the afternoon, but she was always happy to play cards.

In Alton, Illinois, when we came to our first set of locks, Dad warned us how dangerous they could be, but he also said how lucky we were to have them. When the first European explorers came to America, they had to face a series of dangerous waterfalls. Later the locks were built to ease boats from one level of the river to another, so they could avoid the rocky falls. Usually, we went through them with other boats. The steel towboats and tall pushers beside us knocked and clanged inside the narrow chute; then the enormous gates closed. As the lockmaster pumped the water out, we'd slowly descend. Then the gates would open again, and everyone would rev up their motors. The last boat out faced a torrent of swirling waters, so usually the lockmasters put our little boat at the head of the line.

Sometimes while we were waiting for enough boats to fill the locks, we'd be invited aboard one of the tow boats. The first time this happened, the captain of the *White Swan* asked if we wanted to take a shower, and I couldn't wait. What a luxury it was to feel warm water running over my body, to shampoo my hair, and dry it with a clean thirsty towel. Afterwards, in the gleaming, stainless steel galley, we feasted on roast beef and homemade apple pie. The deckhands on the boats, muscular roustabouts, big-shouldered adolescent runaways, and old men with faces as wavy as the river bottom worked three weeks on and one week off, so they missed the company of women. This made them very flirtatious. Their language was rough, but they had many colorful stories about the river to share. "Just like in Mark Twain's day, kids," Mom said, "These men know this river like the back of their hands. Dad can learn a lot from them."

The weather in October wobbled between glorious and miserable. On sunny days autumn trees blazed with color and the blue sky overhead filled with birds flying south, but cold fronts were common. Small wavelets stirred the usually calm river then, and we'd haul out our sweaters. Some mornings the river steamed with fog, making the banks barely visible, but every mile achieved brought new sights, smells and sounds. As we steamed past farmlands, past small towns with silos, someone on a houseboat would wave. The sweet smell of gasoline from passing barges was perfume to our noses. At night the low moan of our anchor rode straining to hold us in place sounded like a lullaby. Like a snake shedding its skin, any reluctance I had about believing in Dad's dream unraveled. As we drifted past mile-marker after mile-marker, the slow movement of the river seemed to sweep time away. There was only the here and now, the river flowing southward, birds we'd never seen before, and a sky full of promise.

Camping was a common event when we were little, and one of our favorite spots was Starved Rock on the Illinois River. When we passed it, Dad called everyone on deck. "There it is!" he said. "Remember being up on top of that bluff?"

According to the legend, a massacre occurred there in the 1700s after a group of Illiniwek Indians killed Pontiac, chief of the Ottawas. At some point allies of the Ottawas decided to avenge the chief's death. During one of the fierce fights that followed, a large group of Illiniwek braves were driven to the top of a 125-foot high sandstone bluff. The Potawatomi held them there so long some of them starved. When it became clear there was no way out, many of the young braves chose to leap off the sandstone bluff, to end their lives nobly, rather than surrender to their enemies.

Far above our heads, Starved Rock looked different, but as we swirled past it, I could still imagine young braves peeling off the edge of the cliff, floating down like brown autumn leaves onto the rocks below.

As cold winds pushed us south, Dad spent most of his time worrying about navigation problems. Every day unpredictable sandbars and snags threatened to put us aground, damage our propeller, or even puncture the *Elizabeth's* strong hull. Rogue barges were also a problem. Having come loose from their pushers, the rusty iron monsters would come sweeping down the river at great speed, usually ending with their blunt maws shoved against a nearby riverbank.

The Army Corps of Engineers was supposed to maintain a depth of nine feet in the channel, but rivers are living entities with minds of their own. It didn't take much of a drought or a shifting of sand to turn a nine-foot channel into a shallow six-foot hazard. Before we left Chicago, many people had warned Dad about the depth of the river. The *Elizabeth* drew seven feet, so they figured it was inevitable that we'd go aground.

In the olden days, every time a boat had to leave the deep channel, one of the deck hands sounded the bottom with a sounding lead, an old fashioned cylinder with an indentation in the bottom packed with wax. The wax made it possible to know if the river bottom was mud, sand, or rock. Attached to the lead weight was a thin rope, light enough to throw a long way. In a musty old hardware store in Peoria, Illinois, Dad saw a sounding lead languishing in a tin bucket behind a coal stove.

"Ain't sold one of them in quite awhile." The clerk wheezed.

"We draw seven feet," Dad said.

"Man, that's awfully deep. You'll be glad you got this."

"We'll need some beeswax, too."

"If I was you, I'd buy me some toilet rings. The wax in them works just the same as beeswax and costs a heck of a lot less. I always carry a couple boxes on my boat. In case of a leak, that stuff's amazing. It'll plug up holes as big as your thumb."

Dad chuckled as we carried our supplies back to the boat. "Fishermen know all the tricks to save money. There's yachtsmen's style and fishermen's style. We're going fishermen's style."

Dad and I went over the sounding procedure a dozen times. I'd run up to the bow while he stayed at the wheel ready to slam the boat in reverse. As we inched toward the shore, I'd throw the lead-line far out in front of me; then wait until the boat moved over it. *Thunk. Thunk. Thunk.* Small pieces of different colored tape marked the depth.

Nine feet, eight feet...Stop! Hold it there!"

Being the official sounder made me feel important. The boat was our home, and everything we owned was aboard it. If we lost the boat, we'd lose everything.

As we floated through southern Illinois, Gale and I scanned the chart book every day. Like studying geography in school, we enjoyed reading the names of the towns along the river. Some were familiar ones: Marseilles, Peru, Peoria, Pekin, and Havana. Mom said they'd been named by people who had traveled the world or just admired Old World cities. Peering into an old atlas Mom provided, we discovered historic facts about the towns, who settled them and how many people lived there. We never saw the center of the smaller towns because there wasn't enough water for us to approach them, but an increase in buildings along the riverbanks and an occasional HOME COOKED MEALS sign announced they were there. The sweet smell of wood smoke hung in the air, hinting at cabins set back in the woods, and I couldn't help but wonder what kind of people lived there. Were they, like us, full of heady dreams? Or working sun-up to sun-down just to make ends meet?

"This is better than TV!" Tim said, as he watched the river banks swirling past.

"I told you!" Dad grinned. "No way to be bored out here. There's something new around every bend."

Mom was also thrilled. She kept saying how lucky she was to get a chance to have such a great adventure. Every afternoon, if the weather was nice we ate lunch on deck.

One day a whole flock of mallard ducks came whizzing alongside us. "Wow!" Tim screamed. "Look at them go. "

What is freedom? Freedom is life without a time clock. Freedom is never having to worry about what you're wearing or having to be careful what you might say because your neighbor might not like you. Freedom is being able get up every morning knowing you have the whole day to do exactly what you want to do. It's going to bed when you feel tired and waking after you're rested. It's letting the song in your heart out, full and spontaneous. Freedom is being captain of your own ship of life, able to sail to that place just beyond the horizon. It's not having to go to school. It is sitting on a dock all afternoon waiting for a fish to bite. It is sailing into a sunset as red as fire, then watching jukebox colors glow and fade along the horizon. It is being alone with nature--the greatest teacher of all--on a river old as time. As the *Elizabeth* puttered farther and farther south, I felt freer and freer from the past, from all the complications of living on land. I came to understand why Dad had invested so much in a dream everybody thought was crazy. Freedom made me feel real. For the first time in a long time, I was completely happy.

Just before Grafton, Illinois, Mom asked us kids to join her on the stern of the boat. Sitting cross-legged on deck beside her, we could tell by the trance-like look on her face, something exciting was about to happen.

"Any minute now," she said, "we'll be entering the Mississippi River. I just want to remind you kids to be careful when you're on deck. The eddying pools in this river can suck things down in them. They say an extra big eddy once swallowed a steamboat so fast, when she went down her smokestacks were still spitting sparks."

Timmy shifted his butt closer to Gale, but Mom just squared her shoulders and smiled. "Don't worry. That's not going to happen to us. If we pay homage to King Al, the big black alligator that rules over the river, we'll be fine."

Mom's eyes scanned the river nervously.

"King Al wears a golden crown and smokes a white clay pipe. If he gets mad, he can whip this river into a fury, making those eddies swirl. That's why the slaves used to pay homage to him. They knew King Al had a strong hankering for tobacco, so they used to throw plugs of it into the water. Every evening at sun-down, King Al comes to the surface of the river to see who is traveling there. They say you can tell when he's around because the water turns purple. If King Al likes your tobacco, he'll sink back down into his parlor to smoke, and the river will grow quiet again. He has a big red throne-chair down there."

Ordering us to stand, Mom rummaged around in her jacket pocket a minute, then pulled out three wax paper packets and handed each of us one. "We'll be coming to the Mississippi River in a few minutes," she said. "Some people think King Al is just a myth the slaves made up. We, however, are not going to take any chances."

A few minutes after Mom's speech, Dad shouted, "There it is! I can see the buoy now. The start of the Mississippi is straight ahead."

When Mom saw a slight change in the color of the water, she held her hands out straight in front of her. Her body shook and her fingers fluttered. "Okay, kids. Throw your tobacco now!"

As we watched our little packets float astern, Mom cupped both her hands around her mouth. "Please listen, good King Al. We are here to pay homage to you, to ask permission to travel on your river. We're just a hardworking little family hoping to make it to the South Sea Islands. Please enjoy our tobacco. Consider it a token of our great admiration. We're asking you for safe passage."

"Do you think he heard us?" Tim's eyes were glued on the river.

"Of course, he did," Mom said. "Didn't you hear that big thump under the boat?"

When Gale let out a loud snort, Mom glared at her. "Please don't make fun of King Al," she said. "This is serious business."

Coming into St. Louis, the current flowed so fast it felt like we were flying. Towboats pushing loads that were seven barges long and four abreast plowed up and down the river with pleasure vessels weaving between them. When Dad saw a boat dock next to the Eads Bridge, he swung the *Elizabeth* around to bring her bow into the current. Then he "walked" her sideways to make a perfect landing. After we secured her, I stepped ashore, but the ground beneath my feet started to sway. Weaving around like a drunken sailor, I felt like I was going to fall over. Dad grabbed my shoulder. "I see you've earned your sea-legs," he said.

Dressed in khaki pants, a military shirt with epaulets and a pith helmet, the owner of the Mound City Boatyard rushed down to meet us. Spying Gale and me, he crooned in a thick German accent, "Such leetle darlinks. Give me a leetle kiss." Rolling watery blue eyes, he fondled our shoulders and stroked our cheeks. It was obvious the Colonel adored little girls, but Gale and I hated his fawning attention.

Because the Colonel hired Dad to paint the long sign above the marina, we stayed in St. Louis three weeks. One evening coming home from a walk on the levee, my sister and I decided to cut through an empty shed. Halfway through it, we heard a noise, so Gale grabbed my hand. For some reason, whenever we felt scared, Gale and I always sang "Onward Christian Soldiers" at the top of our lungs. I still have no idea where we picked that up, but we truly believed it shielded us from harm. We had just started to duck beneath the bow of a canvas-covered ship on a cradle, when a blaze of light blinded us. Like jacked deer, we froze in our tracks.

"It's him!" Gale said.

Behind the blur of his flashlight, I saw the dome of his pith helmet.

"Run!" I whispered. "Run!" And, so we did. Flying through the dark, we headed for the dim opening at the other end of the shed.

Sprinting after us, the Colonel shouted, "No! No! My leetle darlinks. Don't run away! Stop!"

Whenever my father plied his artistic trade, people gathered around to watch, and he met a lot of people that way. One day a bystander offered to drive the whole family into the city to go grocery-shopping. Did we want to go? The crew of the *Elizabeth* begged Dad to say yes.

The market that spread before us sold everything from vegetables to pots and pans, so we stocked up on everything. In the back seat, on the way home, Gale and I poked through the grocery bags. One of them obviously wasn't ours, because it contained several cartons of Lucky Strike cigarettes. Smoking was a secret vice of mine, so I nudged Gale. When I saw she was nodding and smiling, I thrust my hand into the bag and shoved a carton under my jacket.

After we got back to the boat, Dad handed each of us a bag of groceries and slammed the car door.

"Thanks a lot, Sheriff!"

Sheriff?

Visions of handcuffs and a dank jail cell haunted me all afternoon, but the sheriff never came back. A few hours later, standing under the bridge, I enjoyed my smuggled smokes. As the river that was "too thick to drink and too thin to plow" rolled past, I remembered Mom telling us about all the gamblers and hucksters on the Mississippi River of old. Feeling a kinship with those nefarious folks, I blew a few perfect smoke rings. Then, reaching out to catch one, I thrust my thumb smack in the center of that drifting halo.

During our stay in St. Louis, I did everything I could to avoid the lecherous Colonel. Hunkered down in my bunk, I filled my sketch books with drawings of women's faces, and I also practiced tying nautical knots: sheepshanks, bowlines, half-hitches, square knots--a sailor's life could sometimes depend on a good knot

I also read *Cradle of the Deep*, a historical novel I'd found in a bookstore in Beardstown. It was about a ten-year-old girl in the 1880s who had gone to live on a whaling ship with her father after her mother died. The girl's aunts wanted to take the child ashore to make a proper lady out of her, but she begged her father to let her stay on the boat. The crew, a jovial bunch of rascals, doted on the kid, especially the cook. One day he told her his pea soup would "put hair on her chest," so she religiously started slurping the stuff down. The disappointment she felt when she pulled her shirt up every night made me laugh out loud. Eventually, her aunts did drag her ashore, but she horrified their prim and proper friends by spitting in public and swearing like a pirate. A few months later, they decided she would never be socially acceptable, so they let the girl return to her life at sea. I'd never heard of any other girl being raised on a boat, so I loved Joan Lowell's main character.

The week before we left St. Louis, Mom bought tickets to go aboard the *Goldenrod,* a famous old showboat. We found her slumped against the red brick levee like a tipsy old dowager, but with her tall smokestacks and big paddlewheel, she was still a golden symbol of the Mississippi River's romantic past.

As our family joined the throngs of other people flowing up the showboat's wide gangplank to calliope music, Mom told us the *Goldenrod* was the biggest showboat ever built. She could carry 1,400 people, and in her heyday sported an amazing 2,500 electric lights. Mom's hands flew to her chest. "Just look at her, girls! Imagine how excited people in those small river towns must have been when she came steaming around the bend."

In the grand salon of the *Goldenrod*, we quickly found our seats. The play was *Driven from Home*, a simple story about a family facing eviction. In front of an ancient hand-painted canvas, we saw a pathetic little family huddled together in a gas-lighted parlor. The grey-haired mother sat in a chair sobbing as her husband admitted he once again didn't have enough money to pay the rent. Standing at the edge of the stage, a blonde be-wigged daughter wearing too much make-up, twisted a hanky in her hands and rolled her eyes. The audience moaned. When the black-coated, mustachioed landlord knocked at the door, they started to hiss and boo. Boom! Boom! Boom! They stomped their feet on the floor so hard I feared the planks beneath us might break. We joined in, of course, enjoying the freedom to shout at the villainous man.

After the performance, Captain Bill Menke, already a legend on the river, made a big fuss over me. He was a flirtatious old coot, but still virile and attractive enough to make me swoon when he kissed my hand. Pulling me aside, he put his arm around my waist and whispered in my ear, "When you grow up, you come back here, and I'll give you a job."

Thrilled by the captain's sly offer, I took his promise seriously. It felt good to know if I ever wanted to run away, I had someplace to go.

The night before we left St. Louis, Dad invited Stanley Olsen, a man who spent every day grinding away on his black steel-hulled motorboat, to dinner. Stanley always wore coveralls, a pair of lime green goggles, and a black ski mask to protect him from flying specks of paint. Only his small beak nose and dark darting eyes were visible. Stanley impressed Dad with the work he was doing, so they quickly became friends. Mom, however, didn't like Stanley Olsen.

"I really wish you hadn't asked him, Edward."

"Why, Marie?"

"I don't know. There's something about that guy that gives me the willies."

Dad rolled his eyes. "That's ridiculous, Marie! You don't even know the man."

Mom pouted. "I don't want to either."

Dad looked at me and shrugged. "Whatever you do, Carole, don't grow up to be a woman."

When Stanley arrived that night, I hardly recognized him. All pink-skinned and clean, he'd slicked his hair back so tight it looked like paint. Carrying a shopping bag and a bouquet of roses, he descended the doghouse ladder.

"Welcome aboard," Dad said.

When he handed her the roses, Mom fussed over them like a teenager accepting a prom corsage. "I hope you like meat loaf, Stanley?"

Two rows of tiny yellow rat-teeth glistened in our guest's mouth. "I love meat loaf!" After Timmy, Gale, and I had rotated around the U-shaped dinette booth to make room for him, he sat down.

During dinner, Stanley and Dad discussed boats. Obviously captivated by the romance of Dad's dream, Stanley asked a number of questions. Wasn't it hard on us kids? Wasn't Mom scared one of us might get hurt?

Mom shuddered. "Of course not! It's a wonderful life for the children. Edward is a very experienced sailor."

Tim and Gale and I felt flattered that Stanley included us in the grown-up conversation. He said Gale was pretty, he let me show him some of my fancy new knots, and he didn't even flinch when Tim, always a little over-friendly, kept stroking his hair. Mom had told him a million times to stop touching people's hair, but Tim could never resist.

During dessert, a plump apple pie with a dollop of ice cream, Mom asked Stanley what he did for a living.

"I'm an undertaker." He grinned. "I do people in natural settings." Pulling a black leather binder from his bag, Stanley blushed. "As a matter a fact, I just happen to have my portfolio of pictures with me."

"An undertaker?" Mom took a step backward. "Natural settings?"

Setting his big black book in the middle of the table, Stanley drew his long fingers lovingly over its embossed black and gold cover. "Sure," he said. Opening the book, he flipped through the plastic-covered pages. "See this man? He was a wealthy businessman who grew prize dahlias. A passionate gardener."

In the black-and-white photograph, a man wearing blue jeans, a short-sleeve plaid shirt, and a broad-brimmed straw hat leaned against a picket fence. He held a hose in one hand and a trowel in the other. In front of him, a row of sunflowers leaned beside a tree full of apples.

"It's a specialty." Stanley grinned. "It really means a lot to the families."

Tim pushed closer to see, but Gale grabbed him by the arm. Mom looked like she expected Stanley to any minute jump up to fling a measuring tape around her waist. "Oh, my," she said, inching closer to get a better look, "I've never heard of such a thing."

"I've done a lot of celebrities, too." Stanley flipped through more pages, until he came to a picture of a young woman perched pertly on a swing. She wore a fancy white dress. Her legs, frilly with Bo-Peep lace pantaloons, stuck straight out in front of her. The ropes of the swing were covered with heavy vines and roses. Leaning way back, so that her long curls fell almost to her waist, the woman's tiny black shoes pointed toward the sky.

"Do you recognize her?" Stanley asked.

I stared at the woman a long time, but I had no idea who she was.

"Is it Mary Pickford?" Mom asked.

Stanley chuckled. "No, not her, but you're close. She died before her career really took off. An accident of some sort. She was in a lot of pictures, though. Her name was Sylvia LaMonte."

Before Stanley left, he said he was leaving St. Louis the next day, but he hoped we'd all meet again downriver. He promised if we did, he'd buy us a steak dinner.

"Watch out for me," he chuckled, as he went back up the companionway ladder. "I'll be right behind you."

As soon as he was out of earshot, Mom threw her dishtowel down. "See! I told you there was something creepy about that guy! Do you think those people were really dead, Edward? How could he get them to stand up?"

"Wires and props, probably. The farmer was leaning on his rake. I suppose he wired the girl's hands to the swing." Dad chuckled. "But don't worry. I'm sure he's harmless. Who says we have to be laid out all stiff and wearing a black suit anyway? I thought it was a pretty clever idea."

That night I had trouble falling asleep. Images of Dad standing in some funeral parlor with a steering wheel in his hand swirled around my bunk. Mom would, of course, be in a kitchen, probably wearing a polka-dot dress with a frilly, white apron over it, maybe bending over to peer into an oven.

After we left St. Louis, Gale and I breathed a sigh of relief. Escaping the lecherous advances of the Colonel meant we could relax, but the next few days proved to be miserable. Torrential rains and forty-degree temperatures kept everyone but Dad inside the stuffy cabin. Timmy was restless, Gale and I started bickering, and Mom seemed edgy. The next big town we were supposed to come to was Cairo, Illinois, the place where the Ohio River flowed into the Mississippi. Dad said we needed gas, but in order get to the dock that sold it, we'd have to go up the Ohio about a mile. We were only a few miles away from the junction of the rivers when the rain finally stopped. "Hooray!" Hoping to get off the boat awhile, Mom and us kids pulled on sweatshirts and sweaters and hurried on deck.

The wind was strong, and black clouds scudded overhead. Dad pointed to the chart on his lap. "I don't know if we can get there before dark. Maybe we should anchor while it's still light."

Gale and I whined like two un-oiled gears. "No. No! Come on, Dad! We want to go into town!" But our pleading outcry only made Dad shoot us "the look," a special grimace designed to let us know he'd raised a crew of idiots.

Standing with my arms folded tightly across my chest, I pretended not to notice. "If we're going to stop, I need to know now," I said impatiently. "I need to wash up and change clothes."

Dad frowned. "Look girls, I know you want to go ashore. I'm sure your mother does too, but it's always safety first on a boat. We'll be fighting the current the whole way, and that will take more gas. Our battery is low, too. I don't want to run out of gas in the dark. Besides, it could start raining again."

When we got to the place where the Ohio met the Mississippi, dusk drew its curtain across our bow. Heavy turbulence grabbed the *Elizabeth*, twisting and turning her in a confusion of currents. When we turned upstream, the boat's engine screamed louder and louder. Dad tried to swing over to the edge of the channel to get out of the current, but night was closing in fast. Pounding upstream, we noticed the river was rushing wildly, right up to the top of its banks.

*Thump...thump...thump...*every now and then something hard banged against the bottom of our hull. "What the heck is going on?" Dad groaned "There's an awful lot of debris in this river."

As the sky turned from grey to black, it seemed clear we might not make it to the gas dock, but anchoring in such a furious current was out of the question.

"Look!" Dad peered ahead. "I see the bridge! The gas dock is right beyond it." Bending down to check the gauge, Dad tapped it a few times and frowned. "It's almost on E."

By the time we reached the bridge, we could see lights up ahead, but looking up at the iron struts and railroad ties above us, we realized we were barely moving.

"I knew this was a bad idea." Dad pursed his lips. "You girls could have waited until morning to go into town."

When we finally drew abreast of the gas dock, two men appeared. One of them wore a red silk bomber jacket, the other a full set of oilskins with high black boots. They were waving their arms at us, shouting, "Go back! Go back!"

Dad yelled between cupped hands. "I can't! I'm almost out of gas."

Dad swung the *Elizabeth* around, but the powerful current made it hard to control her. By the time we reached the dock, pitch black darkness had descended. After catching our lines, the two men rushed forward. "Better be quick." The man with the red jacket grabbed the gas hose out of its socket. "Fill her up, and then take right off. The river is flooding. It won't crest until midnight. This dock won't hold. "

After our tank was full, Frank told us he was the dock master. "Come with me," he said. "I want to show you something."

Dad and I followed him up a long iron ladder mounted on a wheelhouse situated at the end of the barge that housed the gas dock. After we stepped inside, Frank led us to a big wood-framed window in front of a huge steering wheel. When he flicked a switch, a powerful beam of light illuminated the river below.

"Holy cow!" Dad's eyes squinted as he tried to see how far the writhing, churning log-jam stretched, but there was no end to it, only hundreds of trees bobbing and surging with the river current. Inside the churning, bubbling mass, we saw a chicken coop and a twisted sign advertising John Deere tractors. Bumping and groaning like eager racehorses ready to spring out of a starting gate, hundreds of logs were pushed up against a thirty-foot tree that had slid crossways against the cable that held the gas dock to shore.

Frank flicked the switch off and shook his head. "That cable could break any minute. If it does, it'll take the whole dock with it. "

Dazed by what we'd seen, Dad and I hurried back to the boat, but Mom had already heard about the danger.

"What are we going to do, Edward?"

Hunched on the companionway ladder, Dad looked worried. "Well, we can't leave the boat, Marie. We can't risk losing her. The *Elizabeth's* hull is strong. I think we'll just have to ride it out."

Interrupting Mom and Dad's tense conversation, heavy footsteps landed on our deck. When Dad shoved the companionway hatch open, Frank stood there. The red silk fabric on his jacket sleeves flapped like dozens of little flags. "Better get your wife and kids off that boat. A car is coming for mine. I'm sending them to the Sailfish Motel down the road. Yours better go with them."

Mom looked at Gale. Gale looked at Timmy, and Timmy looked at me. Then we all looked at Dad. Visions of a warm motel room teased me, but I already knew what Dad's answer would be.

"Gee thanks. I appreciate the offer." Dad grinned. "But we're going to ride it out here. I don't want to leave the boat alone."

Thump, thump, thump…

Frank shook his head. "One of those hull inspectors is going to smash right through your hull. If that log jam breaks, none of you will live to tell about it."

Mom grabbed Dad's arm, but he slammed the hatch shut. "Don't worry, Marie. We'll be fine. Why don't you take Gale and Tim into our bunk? I know you must be tired. By the time you wake up, I bet the sun will be shining. We'll go into town."

Thump, thump, thump...

"I want you to put some warm clothes on, Carole," Dad said. "I'll need your help on deck."

As I pulled on my winter jacket, little pinpricks of excitement shot through my body. A real flood! And Dad was depending on me.

As he and I came pushing out of the companionway, the wind blew harder than ever. The turbulent water rushing past the *Elizabeth's* hull made a high-pitched hissing sound. Bent against the wind, I watched Dad crab his way along the deck. When he came back, he handed me a boat hook. "If one of those big logs breaks loose, we'll have to fend off. Remember one hand for you, and one for the boat. If you fall in the water, the current will sweep you downstream. I'll never be able to get you back on board."

I was standing there contemplating that statement, when a horrible gurgling noise erupted right next to me. Peering into the darkness, I saw a twenty-foot tree shoot from the water. It just stood there, spinning on end for what seemed forever; then it fell backwards into the water, drenching me with cold spray. As it drifted toward the boat, Dad hoisted his boat hook to his shoulder. Poised like that on the edge of the cap-rail, dressed in the green fur-trimmed parka he'd found at the Army Surplus store in Chicago, he looked fierce as an Eskimo about to harpoon a whale. A surge of adrenaline coursed through my body as I flew to his side. Shoving my own hook against the writhing tree, I was surprised by the weight of it, but slowly it started moving. Its gnarled branches cracked and exploded when they hit the *Elizabeth's* hull. Down below, I heard Mom scream, "Edward! Edward!"

Bending over the ventilator above her bunk, Dad shouted into its cupped hood. "It's all right, Marie. It's okay. Everything is under control."

Pushing me toward the stern of the boat, Dad faced the wind. "We better get ready for another one, Carole. It looks like that log jam might have shifted."

A few minutes later, I heard him shout. "Heads up, here comes another one!" This time the tree came up right under the boat, thudding against her bottom like a battering ram. Realizing it was going to surface too close to use my boat hook, I grabbed the handrail on the cabin top to brace myself for what was coming next, but Dad wasn't about to give up. Throwing all his weight against it, he grabbed the tree with his bare hands. Locked in mortal combat, wrestling with the rolling and twisting tree, he somehow managed to keep it away from the hull. When he got to the bow, he shoved the tree away, then hurried back to meet the next one. A deep feeling of awe made my heart race. My father was like Superman, capable of anything.

All that night, Dad and I worked side-by-side in a choreography that became surprisingly easy: thrust, jab, waltz the log to the bow, then run back to the stern. It wasn't until the sky started to show faint streaks of light that the trees came less frequently and the river current slowed.

Finally able to take a break, we sat down. The adrenaline that had kept me going all night faded quickly. All I could think about was sleep.

"It'll be light soon," Dad said, "I'm taking her up a slough I found on the chart. We'll anchor there. Get ready to untie our lines."

Mom opened the hatch and popped her head out.

"Is it over?"

"Yes, it's over, Marie. I told you we'd be fine."

As we puttered toward the slough, random logs still bounced into us, but the current had slowed, leaving an undulating mass of sour smelling debris along the shoreline. After we anchored, I slumped down on the deck to rest my back against the cabin.

"Don't fall asleep yet," Dad said. "I need to take the dinghy into town to get some engine oil. Someone's got to keep watch. We should be safe here, but you never know."

Because I'd been cold all night, the sun felt soft as a blanket. The water gently lapping at the hull sounded like music.

The next thing I knew, Dad was shaking me. "Wake up, Carole. Wake up!"

I rubbed my eyes. "What? Oh, Dad. I fell asleep. I'm sorry."

"That's okay, Carole. You must be exhausted."

Dad helped me to my feet and gave me a big hug. "I was so proud of you last night. I couldn't have asked for a better crew."

After we survived the flood, Mom gave much of the credit to the tribute we'd given King Al. In fact, she was downright smug about it.

"Aren't you glad now," she said, "that we gave him that tobacco?"

Top (l-r) Dad, Mom, Gale, a friend of Gale's
Bottom (l-r) Me, Tim, and Joe

Chapter Four

AFTER THE FLOOD, a renewed sense of pride buoyed our spirits. As the days passed, we grew to love the Mississippi River, the great "Father of Waters" that would take us all the way into the Deep South, all the way to the Gulf of Mexico. We were no longer Chicagoans. We weren't even Northerners anymore. We were river people, adventurers anointed by rushing waters and ready for the Promised Land. Dad hummed at the wheel, and Mom enjoyed keeping a daily log. In every little town we visited, reporters arrived to take our picture, and other boating people clambered aboard to hear our stories. I learned then the power of dreams, how when a person has one, others seem compelled to help make it come true. The people we met along the river invited us to dinner. They shared beers with my parents and listened in awe as my father unveiled his plans. They gave Gale and I books to read, and sat Timmy on their laps. In towns that had yacht clubs or gun clubs, we were invited to use their facilities. Everywhere we went, people treated us like celebrities.

A few days before Memphis, Mom made a big deal about the fact that we were going to experience culture shock.

"Southerners aren't loud like Northerners; they're polite and proud. Some of them haven't got over the Civil War either. They took a terrible beating. You'll hear people say *The South will rise again*, and some still fly the Confederate flag. If you hear anyone calling us "damn Yankees", don't take it personal. People are the same everywhere. You treat them nice, and they'll treat you nice."

Mom was reading *Andersonville* and her sympathy for the South often brought tears to her eyes.

"They were mostly volunteers, you know, farm hands that dropped their plows to walk all the way North to fight for a cause they believed in. Some of those poor kids were only twelve years old. They didn't even have shoes."

After Cairo, the Mississippi widened and the current slowed. The air smelled different, too. Mom swore she could already smell the Gulf of Mexico's humid vapors. Like a slow moving snake, the river slid toward the rich bottomlands of the Delta, shifting its shape as it had for thousands of years, and with every move it made, lives changed.

Armed with her stacks of history books and maps, Mom showed us old towns that had been abandoned when the river decided to loop away from them. These big loops, called oxbows, created islands where none had been before, and along the new riverbeds, towns sprung up. That's what made navigation so hard. Like a living thing, the river coiled and uncoiled according to whim. Snags, changes in the current, rocks, and sandbars appeared and disappeared daily. The Army Corps of Engineers was in charge of mapping the river, but the charts they printed only came out every few years. As Mark Twain pointed out, "The Mississippi River will always have its own way; no engineering skill can persuade it to do otherwise..."

One night just after New Madrid, Dad steered the *Elizabeth* out of the channel so we could anchor. In the quickening dark, I had to squint to see the lead line, but we found eight feet of water. Turning the motor off, he rushed forward to drop the anchor. As usual, we both stood there waiting for the line to snap tight.

"I think we'll be fine here," he said, "but we better keep our eyes open. It could drag."

After enjoying a hearty macaroni and cheese dinner, we sat around the dinette listening to Mom tell us about Graceland, Elvis Presley's famous mansion. Gale and I were giggling and laughing about that, when Dad stood up. Peering through the portlight over the dinette table, he looked worried.

"Come on, Carole," he said. "She's dragged all right. We're sitting right in the middle of the channel. Better get that anchor up and move to a safer spot. "

In the dark, it was impossible to see the marks on the lead line, so Dad ran aft to get a flashlight. As I stood there waiting, a bright light penetrated the trees on shore. In the sky long rays fidgeted across low-lying clouds. Not knowing what they were, I called out to Dad, but he said they were just lights from a pusher upriver.

"They're headed our way. They look close, and by land they would be, but there's a big bend in the river, so they're still miles away. Let's get that anchor up. If we stayed here, the pilot wouldn't see us until he came around that bend. By that time, it'd be too late. There's no way to stop those things."

After we hauled the anchor up, Dad steered the boat out of the channel. Putting her bow to the current, he asked me to take the wheel.

"Head slowly for the riverbank," he said. "I'll get the anchor ready to drop again."

After Dad was sure we were safe, he waved me to the bow.

"We can't get any closer to the shore," he said. "Let's drop her down here."

The anchor splashed into the water, but the line didn't stiffen directly below us. Instead, it stretched aft. As the *Elizabeth* slowly drifted back into the channel, Dad's flashlight scanned the throbbing line. When he saw the anchor bobbing on top of the water, his eyes opened wide. "What the heck? I've never seen anything like that!" he said. "The current is so strong; it's keeping it from sinking!"

By the time the anchor finally did sink, we were back in the channel again.

"Come on," he shouted, racing to the bow. "We've got to get that thing up!" Dad and I bent forward and pulled as hard as we could, but the anchor wouldn't budge.

"It must be snagged on something." Dad groaned.

"Can't you call them on the radio?"

"No. The damn transmitter died back in Cairo," Dad said. "The receiver is still okay, so we'll be able to hear them, but we can't call out."

Hearing our tense voices, Mom popped her head out of the hatch.

"What's going on?"

"We've got a problem, Marie. The current dragged the anchor back in the channel, and we can't get it up. Go get the floodlight. It's in a black box in the tool room. Hurry! If we shine it up in the air, at least they'll know someone is here."

Long before we actually saw the pusher, the ominous rumble of its powerful propellers rolled over us. When Mom brought the floodlight on deck, Dad set it up for her. "Just shine it up in the air," he said. "I'm going below to see if I can hear them on the radio." A few minutes, later we heard the radio sputter and come alive. "This is the *Bright Star* calling *Miss*

Lucy .... Yuh, see that, Mike! .... Some damn fool's anchored right in the channel... Some yacht from Chicago."

As the brilliantly-lit pusher veered as far away from us as it could, the *Elizabeth* surged sideways. We could see the pilot in the wheelhouse looking down on us.

"This is the *Bright Star* calling the yacht *Elizabeth*. Hey, Cap, you better get the hell outta there! You wanna get killed?"

Mom and Dad stayed up all night, shining our light in the sky so the pushers would know we were there. By the time I went below, Gale was asleep, and Tim was in my bunk. Crawling next to my little brother, I bumped my arm against his shoulder.

"Is everything okay, Carole?"

"Sure," I said. "Go back to sleep."

"Will you rub my back?" he asked.

"Okay, but go to sleep. I'm tired."

The next morning when Dad woke me, it was barely light. After gulping down quick cups of coffee, we headed for the bow. We expected to have a hard time getting the anchor up, but this time it came loose on the first try.

Later that afternoon, Dad opened his chart book. "I'm going to stop in Caruthersville. It's the first town in Missouri and not very far. Maybe they'll have a marine store. I need to find a heavier anchor."

After we dropped the hook in Caruthersville, Dad and I got in the dinghy and rowed into town. There wasn't much of anything there, not even a hardware store within walking distance, so we started trudging along the riverfront. Eventually we met a guy working on a small fishing boat, a friendly man with curly, brown hair and the body of a bear. When we said we were looking to buy an anchor, he scratched his head and grinned.

"Reckon I know somebody's got one."

As we bounced along the dusty back roads in Jake's truck, he didn't say a word. I'd gotten used to that. It was obvious Southerners didn't talk much. They always seemed to be mulling things over. Mom said it might be because it was so hot in the South. It did take some effort, after all, to be talking all the time.

Eventually, we pulled in front of a shack only a little bigger than an outhouse. Half-hidden by trees, it leaned to one side. It certainly was colorful, though, because someone had shingled the whole outside with license plates from all over the United States.

Jake opened a torn screen door clinging to the small structure and shouted inside. "Hey, Uncle Bill!" A few minutes

later, a barefoot old man wearing a pair of torn blue jeans came
out. A sickle-shaped scar ran across one of his nipples.

"These folks are goin' down river to New Orleans. They're
lookin' to buy a big anchor. You wanna sell yur'n?"

Shoving a furled Batman comic into his back pocket, Uncle
Bill invited us in.

"Set yurselfs down awhile." He waved his hand toward a
couple of wire milk crates set beside a woodstove with a yellow-
eyed cat napping on top. Every now and then, spitting a stream of
brown liquid into an empty tuna fish can, Uncle Bill took forever
to start talking.

"Well...I don't rightly know if I want to sell her or not. It's
mighty hard to find a big un in these parts. If I ever git me a boat
again, I might need it."

"Can we see it?" Dad asked.

"Yessiree!" Uncle Bill jumped up. "Foller me."

Limping outside into a yard littered with junk, he led us to a
broken-down shed. When he pulled open the door, a squadron
of rats scampered into the woods. Boxes full of all kinds of
antiques lined the walls, and the sour smell of rotting cardboard
and animal droppings saturated the heavy air. We followed him
to the back of the shed through a maze of boxes, until we came to

a big anchor dangling from a rope in front of a dusty cobweb-laden window.

"She's a hundred-fifty pound Danforth," Bill said proudly. "I betcha there ain't anuther one in a hundred miles. Some old river pilot gave me this un. She came from New York City."

"So how much do you want for her?" Dad asked.

Uncle Bill raised one shaggy eyebrow. He pulled on his bottom lip.

"How much ya wanna give me?"

"Well, I don't know," Dad said. "I haven't got a lot of money."

"Hmmm..."

After bending over to spit into a cardboard box full of warped books, Uncle Bill rubbed his hands up and down his legs.

"How, 'bout fifty bucks?"

Dad pointed to a shiny two-burner kerosene stove. "Okay, it's a deal, but can you throw that in too?"

After we were back in the dinghy, I asked Dad why he hadn't offered the old man less money. It wasn't like him not to dicker about price.

"Didn't you see his house, Carole? He obviously needed the cash."

When Dad showed Mom the kerosene stove, she was happy. The farther south we went, the worse the quality of the coal we could buy. Up north, we could get hard anthracite coal, but the peat down south was soft and oily. Thin threads of black smoke poured from Mom's Shipmate, so she was always complaining. Ever since we'd left Illinois, Dad had been looking for alternative fuels.

"See, Marie. You prime it like this." Dad lifted a red kerosene can with a long nozzle above the stove. When he placed the tip of it inside the little cup beneath the burner, Mom looked over his shoulder. Before he lighted the flame, he pumped a small handle up and down. Then he tossed a match at the burner and a nice ring of bright blue flames flared in an even circle.

Mom clapped her hands together. "Nice!"

"Here, now you try it," Dad said.

Mom's hand shook a little when she pointed the nozzle toward the stove. "It's kind of hard to see," she said. Taking off her glasses, she leaned forward. "Where's it go again?"

"Right there. In the little cup, Marie."

It all happened so fast, it was hard to tell what she did wrong, but the next thing I knew, Mom was whirling around the galley screaming. Dad rushed to her side, patting her smoking head with a dishtowel, while I ran toward the galley sink.

When Dad pulled the towel away, Mom's fingertips groped along the ridge where her eyebrows should be.

"Carole, get me a mirror."

"Oh, dear! Oh, Marie! I'm so sorry." Dad tried to hug her, but Mom shoved him away. "I should have known it would be too complicated for you," he said. "I'll buy you a propane stove in Memphis. I promise."

When Mom looked in the mirror, she started sobbing. Black streaks ran down her cheeks. The singed hair above her forehead looked like brown steel wool. "My whole head could have gone up in flames, Edward."

Trying to be consoling, I put my arm around her waist.

"You can borrow my eyebrow pencil," I said. "You've still got a few hairs left."

Mom stared in the mirror a long time; then she pushed past us to crawl into her bunk. It took a lot of coaxing to get her to come out again, but by dinnertime she was once more stoking up the Shipmate. When Mom plunked Dad's plate of pork chops in front of him, she didn't say a word. She didn't even add sugar and cream to his coffee or stir it like she always did.

Dad sipped his coffee. "Your eyebrows look fine, Marie. You can't even tell they're just pencil."

After Mom washed the dishes and cleaned up the galley, she made me help her carry the kerosene stove on deck, where standing on the end of the transom, she gave the offending appliance the *deep-six*.

"If that man says one more word to me about how I look," she said. "I think I'll scream."

Mom and Tim look out the hatch.

Chapter Five

A FEW MILES UPRIVER from Memphis, Mom accelerated her charm-school curriculum. "Please try to keep your voices down, girls. Southern ladies speak very softly. Also, never yell Ma at me. Mom, Mother, or Mama is okay. When you kids start yelling Ma, you sound like a herd of bleating sheep."

Because she was such a history buff, and maybe because we weren't attending school, Mom gathered whatever information she could about the places we visited. As the *Elizabeth* puttered her way south, she taught us a lot about American history, and her lessons weren't dry like the history lessons in school. Mom always had a story to tell. For instance, in Memphis in 1862, a big naval battle took place. Under the command of a flag officer named Charles Davis, several ironclad ships fought to win control of the city. Almost two hundred Confederate soldiers lost their lives in that battle.

"Ironclad ships were a new invention," Mom said. "It was hot as heck inside them, too. Like being dried kidney beans in a tin can. But those iron boats were the only things that could stave off the minie-balls shot from enemy cannons. It was a dreadful scene. Smoke hanging over the river. The cries of wounded men. The smell of blood. Memphis was a decisive battle because the winner could control all the shipping on the river. If the Union held it, the Confederacy knew they wouldn't be able to get arms or supplies to any of their troops in the North. Brother against brother. Gee, Tim, those men fought so hard."

Mom also loved music. "It's where the blues were born," she said. "The songs and rhythms the slaves brought over from Africa started it. The chants they sang as they worked on the river or in the cotton fields were called field hollers. That's where the blues came from. Back in its heyday, field hands, roustabouts, and rivermen used to swarm into Beale Street, but in the 1800s yellow fever struck. It killed so many people, there was hardly anybody left. One guy was smart, though. His name was Robert Church, Sr., and he bought up several abandoned buildings on Beale Street. Talk about wide open! Pickpockets and card sharks were everywhere. Beale Street was so rough, it had its own undertaker, and voodoo flourished. The roustabouts who came to Beale Street wanted to live it up, so the pool halls and saloons were full of gamblers and prostitutes. Everyone was looking to make a buck, and everyone was singing the blues. One day a guy named Handy started writing the music down, and other musicians started playing it. Elvis used to hang around Beale Street. He bought flashy clothes down there, and he picked up on the music he heard. Beale Street was the home of the blues, but rock and roll was born there too. You kids won't be able to go into the bars, of course, but I hope some street musicians are still hanging around."

Mom read heart-wrenching passages from *Uncle Tom's Cabin*, the book that had swayed so many people to become abolitionists. Mom hated slavery, and we did too. How could the slaveholders think it was okay to sell another human being? How could they take small children away from their parents or whip a man until his back bled?

The day we arrived in Memphis, the temperature soared to 60 degrees. Christmas and my fifteenth birthday were only a few weeks away, yet there we were, wearing only light sweaters or no coats at all. Gale's main interest in Memphis was Elvis. I wasn't crazy about him, even though I did like his "Love Me Tender" song. Somewhere in her travels, my sister acquired an autographed blue-and-green striped Elvis Presley shirt with cuffed sleeves and a high black collar. The first week we were there, she never took it off.

The dock we found was within walking distance to town, so we took a bus to Graceland, but the mansion was closed that day, so all we could do was look through the fence decorated with musical notes. "Gee, it's smaller than I expected," Mom said. Gale didn't care. Confident the King himself was going to come out, she made us hang around outside the fence a long time. "I'll get him to autograph my hand." She giggled.

One night I heard Dad say he'd better get a lot of sign-painting jobs in Memphis because he was almost broke. Besides what we needed to live on, gas cost a bundle and the motor needed fixing. All the vibrating it did during the Ohio flood caused a small leak in the place where the propeller shaft went through the hull.

When Dad set out every morning carrying his black leather sign kit, we knew if he found plenty of signs to paint that day we'd have a good dinner. If not it would mean one of Mom's "frugal" meals—usually hot dogs and beans or hamburgers and rice.

"The wages here are so low, Marie. A sign I'd get twenty dollars for in Chicago will only bring ten here. And a lot of people don't trust a stranger to paint their signs either, especially a Yankee."

In December, I decided to get a job. You had to be sixteen to work. I was still only fifteen, but I knew I looked older. By lying about my age and using Mom's Social Security card, I got a job at J.J. Newbury's downtown. Mom said I was a million dollar baby in a five-and-ten cent store. I could tell she was proud of me.

Ralph, the manager, showed me how to run the cash register and wait on customers. My first assignment was in the jewelry department. The dazzling array of rhinestone necklaces, silver bracelets, and dangling earrings glistened and tinkled when I held them.

My co-worker, a fidgety woman named Florence, grabbed all the customers before I could get to them, so all I could do was straighten and re-straighten the rows of merchandise. It took almost a week before she dared leave me alone. "I'll just grab a quick bite at the lunch counter," she said. "If you need anything, come get me."

My first customer, a pretty blonde woman wearing high heels, a ruffled white blouse, and a big puffy skirt, drifted back and forth along the counter. The minute she paused, I jumped forward.

"May I help you?"

She dug around in her green plastic purse a minute. "I'll take a pair of those pearl earbobs, please. Just put 'em in a sack."

Earbobs? A sack? Those were foreign words to me, so I just stood there. To me a sack meant a coal sack or a big brown thing you put groceries in. And *earbobs?* What the heck were earbobs? It took me a few minutes to unravel the mystery. *She had said a pair of pearl ones, right?* All of a sudden, I got it. Grabbing a pair of pearl earrings from the row in front of her, I automatically reached for a bag. *Oh, yeah, a bag must be a sack!"*

"Thank you, baby."

I was still chuckling to myself, when Florence returned.

"How'd it go?" she asked.

"Great!" I said. "I made my first sale."

All that day, I listened to Florence wait on people. I figured if I was going to work and live in the South, I might as well learn how to speak southern, so I practiced on the next few customers. *Yes, Ma'am. Thank you, Ma'am. That'll be $3.00, Ma'am. Y'all come back real soon now. Yuh hear?"*

The day I got my first paycheck, I raced home to grab a notebook. Plopping down on my bunk, I set to work figuring how much money I'd earn before Christmas. Timmy had been dying for someone to buy him a gun and holster set. Mom needed new nylons. Gale would love a book about Indian handicrafts, and Dad could always use a tool. If my sums were correct, I'd be able to buy everyone presents and still have a few dollars left over.

I knew we didn't have much money, so I wasn't expecting anything for my birthday, but Mom did buy me a tiny birthday cake. When Tim tried to put all the candles on it, he got frustrated.

"There's too many!" he said.

Gale laughed. "It looks like a pink porcupine."

I only got a small tin of watercolors and a drawing pad, but I didn't care.

"You're sweet sixteen, a real teenager now," Dad said.

"God help us!" Mom laughed.

School had been a nightmare for me, but work was totally different. I woke up each morning excited about going to my job, and my manager was crazy about me. He said I had a quick mind and was very mature for my age. I blushed, but I knew it was true. The river had made me that way.

Just before Christmas, Ralph had a great idea. Our store had a big record department with a public address system, so because of my clear speaking voice, he set me up like a disk jockey. I'd play a few songs and do a few commercials.

"Attention! Attention! Are there any mothers in the store? Santa Claus is now in the toy department. Come and have your baby's picture taken. It's an heirloom you'll treasure forever."

As the holiday season shifted into high gear, I visited the toy department often. When I saw the shelves were emptying, I grabbed the best holster set I could find--two shiny pistols in black plastic holsters with fancy silver medallions. Sliding them under my counter, I kept picturing Timmy's face when he saw them.

Being an announcer made me feel like a radio celebrity, so I bought myself some fancier clothes. After months of only wearing t-shirts, sweatshirts or blue jeans, it felt good to feel glamorous again. High heels, double ponytails, pink lipstick and heavy eye make-up, Bardot was back, and, man, was she popular. I could hardly handle the swarms of young boys wanting to talk to me. I was feeling sky high, until I found out my paycheck wouldn't come until two days after Christmas. I hadn't saved any money, so how was I supposed to pay for Tim's holster? At first, I felt angry. Didn't the owners of the store realize their hardworking employees might need to get paid before Christmas? I also felt stupid for not knowing this could happen.

Stumbling into Ralph's office, I plunked myself down in a chair.

"What's the matter, baby?"

"I was counting on getting paid before Christmas." Choking on my own words, feeling totally humiliated, I started to cry, so Ralph came over to pat my face with a Kleenex.

"There, there." He said. "Ain't no use in getting so upset."

After I stopped blubbering like a baby, I told him about the holster set. How much I was counting on buying it for my baby brother.

Ralph's mouth drooped, and his eyes looked sad.

"Well, there ain't nothin' I can do about the paycheck. That's company policy, honey, but if it means that much to you,

I'll loan you a few bucks myself. Pay me back when you get your check."

On Christmas morning, when Timmy rushed to look under the tiny tree Mom had put in the main cabin, I felt almost as excited as he did. As he tore through the candy-cane decorated paper, Mom put her hand on my shoulder and squeezed.

"Oh, Carole!" Tim shrieked. "This is just what I asked for! Thank you!"

Gale gushed over her book about Indians. Mom made a big fuss over the nylons, and Dad said the screwdriver I got him was just the size he needed.

Even though I'd been hired as a seasonal worker, Ralph didn't want to let me go after Christmas. He didn't need any more counter help, so he found something else for me to do.

"Hey, wanna paint some mannequins? I found a bunch in the basement that need refreshment."

I enjoyed my work with the dummies. Some were only-half bodied, but others were full-figured. They looked like big naked dolls to me. Carefully drawing thin lines of red paint across their wooden lips or touching a tiny spot of white paint to their black pupils to make their eyes sparkle, I felt like I was bringing them back to life.

After I finished all the mannequins, Ralph moved me into his office. Sitting at a small table in the corner, I stuffed envelopes with flyers, and even did some filing.

One day, he handed me the phone book. "I need you to call Kresge's to place an order for fourteen boxes of white candles and twenty boxes of napkins. Tell them you can't pick the stuff up until 6:30. They'll tell you they close at five, but this is a big order, so I'm sure they'll have somebody stay late. If they say anything, tell them you're having a wedding."

"But why order from them?" I asked. "Don't we sell those things?"

"Oh, we're not really going to buy all that stuff." Ralph chuckled. "I just want to play a joke on Barney, the manager."

I made the call, but when I got home that night, I kept watching the clock, imaging some poor clerk standing beside the loading dock waiting for someone who would never come.

A few days later, Ralph approached me again. This time I was supposed to call the SPCA to act like I was a customer that was all upset over Kresge's dirty pet department.

When I told Dad what I was doing, he hit the roof.

"That's horrible!" he said. "It's against the law. You could end up in jail. You're not going back there."

117

I felt torn. I loved my boss, but I knew Dad was right, so the next day I quit. On my way home, I picked up a newspaper, and I was reading it when Dad came home for lunch.

"There aren't any jobs out there," I said. "They all want references. I know Ralph won't give me one."

Waving his cheese sandwich in my face, Dad told me his secret. "Do what I do," he said. "Walk into town and stop in every single store. Don't miss even one. That's how I get sign jobs. You never know. Somebody might have quit that day. Not all jobs are advertised."

Following Dad's advice, I tried a bakery, a hardware store, and a clothing store. None of them needed anyone, but I finally got hired as a waitress in a Walgreen's drugstore.

Glenn, the acne-faced manager, had sharp cheekbones, bushy eyebrows and side burns that reminded me of Abraham Lincoln's.

"When can you start?"

The best thing about Walgreen's was their training program. Everything had to be done according to a big black book, so I studied it every night. My uniform was cute too, a yellow apron over a green frock with a little chest pocket holding a tiny yellow hanky. I was put on the counter, but hoped to graduate soon to the dining room where everyone said the tips were better. It didn't hurt, of course, that a lot of young businessmen came in there to eat. It didn't take me long to learn that the more I flirted, the faster my apron pockets bulged with cash. Flouncing up and down the counter with my pony-tail bobbing, joking and laughing with the customers, I was amazed at my own efficiency. At night when we counted up our tickets, my pile was always thickest. The old pros that had worked there for a hundred years felt jealous at first, so they pushed me around every chance they got. They gave me the worst side-work and whispered behind my back; not that I cared. I was thrilled to be making so much money.

Being a smart company, Walgreen's had a new promotion every week: 19-cent early bird breakfasts, sundaes priced according to balloons you had to break with a dart, and all-you-could- eat catfish on Fridays. They also had contests based on sales, and I won every time.

One day an old colored man wearing brown pants and a red V-neck sweater came in. When he sat down at the lunch counter and picked up a menu, I got the man's water. I was getting ready to wait on him when Glenn pulled me aside.

"Don't wait on that guy," he said,

"Why?"

"We don't serve niggers here. Some of these boys are trying to cause trouble by sitting down anyway."

It was inconceivable to me that a restaurant could refuse to serve anybody.

"But what am I supposed to do? He knows I already saw him."

"Just ignore him. Pretend he isn't there."

Backing away from the counter, I ducked into a small alcove at the far end of the grill. I kept peeking out to see if the guy was still there, but he stayed a long time. Eventually some white people came in, but when they saw the colored man sitting there, they avoided the lunch counter and swept into the booth area. I was trying to figure out what to do, when suddenly the old man slipped off the stool and disappeared.

One of the waitresses on the floor muttered. "Damn niggers! They got a helluva lot of nerve, coming in here like that." Another slammed her book of checks down on the counter. "It's those damn Yankees riling them up," she said. "They're making them want to vote. Most of them can't even read."

I never went into the kitchen except to punch the time clock. There was no reason to because the Black dishwasher was supposed to bring anything we needed. Leroy was friendly. We were both about the same age, so sometimes when our breaks coincided, we'd sit on the back steps smoking cigarettes. I told him we were from Chicago, just passing through on our way to the South Sea Islands. He said his father was a janitor. Leroy had nine brothers and sisters, and his mother took in laundry. I was reading Hemingway, and he was reading Dr. Martin Luther King. Leroy knew he was cute. His smile was like sunshine over water, and he had the body of an atholete. I liked the way he teased me, so we did a little flirting.

One morning when business was slow, I decided to fill the sugar bowls. There weren't any bags under the counter, so I walked to the kitchen door.

"Hey, Leroy," I yelled. "Bring me some sugar."

A few minute later, Leroy emerged with a big grin on his face. His hips gyrated back and forth, and he was twirling a dish towel.

"Oh, baby, have I got sugar for you."

The next thing I knew Glenn was there, grabbing Leroy by the neck and shoving him back into the kitchen. I followed after them, pulling on Glenn's arm, begging him to stop, but he pushed me away. When he got to the back door, he lifted Leroy by his shirt and pants and threw him sprawling on the ground.

After Glenn came back in, he sat at the lunch counter, angrily ripping the paper off a straw. Slipping onto the stool next to him, I tried to make him understand that Leroy hadn't done anything wrong.

"C'mon, Glenn, Leroy's a good kid. This is all my fault. I'm the one who started it."

Glenn's eyebrows jerked up and down, and his foot was shaking. "You just don't get it," he said. "This ain't the North, so you better learn to leave those nigger-boys alone. You're goddamn lucky I was here. You fool around like that, and one of these nights some niggers going to follow you home. That boy could have raped you."

"Leroy?" I snorted. "That's ridiculous. He's my friend. I know you're mad, Glenn, but please don't fire him. His family really needs the money."

"His ass is already fired." Glenn grunted.

The meanness of Glenn's words shocked me. If more colored people came in, what would I do? There was no way I could just ignore them, so I quit.

Glenn shrugged. "Suit yourself," he said. "You want to be a nigger-lover, it's no skin off my ass."

Taking off my apron, I felt sad. Dad was right. In contrast to all the nice folks we'd met on the river, an abundance of Dreamcrushers lived on land. When I went into the kitchen to punch out, the cooks all glared at me, but now I knew why. After shoving my time-card into its slot and slamming the bar down, I pulled my shoulders back and faced them. "South or no south," I said. "I'll flirt with anybody I want to. If you see Leroy, tell him I'm sorry."

I hated not getting a paycheck, but my parents assured me I'd done the right thing, and Dad was lucky enough to have sold quite a few signs. We were leaving soon, so instead of looking for another job, I joined Mom and the kids on their daily excursions. Big bustling Memphis had a ton of stores, and even though she didn't have enough money to buy anything, Mom liked wandering through them. As we joined the flow of people on the sidewalks, the hurrying crowds rushing across every intersection made me feel like a minnow swimming upstream. Car's beeped. Sirens screamed. It was as if the roar of the city was like one of those eddies Mom had warned us about. I felt sick to my stomach. On the river, wrapped in the security of our family, everything seemed hopeful and exciting. On land, it was all bedlam and bad feelings. I couldn't wait to get back on the river.

Mom was always telling us how genteel the people in the South were, but after what happened with Leroy, I found it hard to agree. One day, when I asked her about this, she gave me a lesson about travel.

"I know how you feel." Mom shook her head in sympathy. "It's terrible to see separate drinking fountains and windows on the sides of restaurants. They can't even go to the show. Colored people have to sit in the balcony here and ride in the back of the bus, but we're just passing through, Carole, so who are we to judge? People in different places have different ways of doing things. In China they used to bind women's feet so tight they could barely walk. In the Middle East, men won't even eat with a woman who has her period, but there are many beautiful things about those places. If you want to travel, you have to learn to overlook local customs. "

I guess there are times in most people's lives when they experience something that can only be called a sacred moment. Ever since my perfect childhood exploded into confusion, I'd wanted to belong, but circumstances had always made me an outsider. For some reason, that day, standing at the end of the

Elizabeth's long bowsprit, watching a line of mallard ducks skim through strands of pink and white morning mist. I felt the river inside me. As the lush riverbank walls enfolded me, I breathed a sigh of relief. It struck me then that it wasn't the world that was wrong; it was the people. As I listened to the gurgle of the river as it flowed past our hull, I suddenly knew, with the blue sky over my head and all of America as my back yard, I did belong. I belonged on the river.

The run from Memphis to Greenville, Mississippi, went smoothly. Our confidence in handling the boat and the slower tempo of the river as it widened into the Delta gave us a chance to relax. As, day after day, we floated farther and father away from the North, Dad's dream of reaching the islands seemed more and more possible.

"Someday soon, kids, we're going to see palm trees."

A few days later, Mom flew into a tizzy when Dad announced we were coming into Greenville, Mississippi, and we'd be staying at the yacht club there. Shifting into high gear, she rummaged through the hanging-locker looking for appropriate clothes. Dad, of course, refused to wear the khaki shirt and pants she had given him for Christmas. I'd only seen my father dressed up once, and that was in a photograph. In it he looked like somebody else wearing a fancy black hat and a navy blue overcoat. Like Jughead in the comics, he always wore the same outfit, a green cotton turtleneck shirt and blue jeans. Mom had been hounding him for years to buy one of those snazzy white captain's caps with a black plastic bill full of gold braid, but he preferred his black watch cap.

A few hours before our arrival, we gathered around the table for Mom's last minute instructions. In serious tones, she made it clear that we were not going to act like a bunch of wild monkeys.

"We taught you kids how to behave so we could take you anywhere and be proud. I expect you to be on your best behavior. That means no bickering, no yelling, and no interrupting us adults when we're talking. Remember, we're yachtsmen," she said, "not a bunch of gypsies."

As Dad circled the boat to bring her up to the dock, we all came on deck. Gale wore a dress someone had given her, an off-the-shoulder sundress with a low-cut neckline, a cinched waist, and a full skirt that ballooned almost to her ankles. Personally, I thought she looked like she was wearing a costume, like one of the actresses on the old *Goldenrod* showboat, but she thought she looked glamorous. Having renewed my wardrobe in Memphis, I chose a tight black skirt, a crisp white blouse, nylons, and black flats. Timmy looked cute in a new yellow shirt. He had his hair all slicked down, but one of the frayed straps on his orange life jacket had broken. He'd been wearing the nasty thing ever since we moved onto the boat, and he'd grown a lot since then. Mom sighed as she pinned it together with a big safety pin. "Look how dirty this thing is. It's disgusting, Tim. Take it off as soon as you're on shore."

When they saw us approaching, a group of yacht club members came down to the dock. Soon our boat was loaded with yacht club dandies wanting to hear all about our trip down the river. One especially nice couple, who had a son and daughter my age, invited us to have supper at their house.

As we walked to the Lowrys', Mom must have used the word *genteel* at least a dozen times.

"They're not royalty, Marie. For God's sake. They're just people. Stop fussing."

When Dad rang the front doorbell, we all checked our appearances. Mom pulled out a compact and applied new lipstick. Then she fluffed up her hair. Gale looked down to make sure her low cut dress wasn't exposing her imaginary cleavage. Tim obviously enjoyed being unharnessed from his lifejacket. He kept rubbing his hands across his chest. Peering through thick beveled glass, Mom pushed her hip against me. "Oh, look!" she cried. "Wouldn't you just know it! They have a chandelier in the front hall."

The Lowrys welcomed us with all the warmth for which Southerners are famous, and Marcia and Kevin treated me like a visiting cousin. After a few minutes of small talk, they took me upstairs to their bedrooms. Planes on the ceiling for Kevin, and a big four-poster canopy bed for Marcia. Complimenting everything I saw, I tried speaking softly, even throwing in a few *y'alls* for effect.

After a formal dinner, complete with white china and a lot of silver platters served by a colored maid named Ruthie, we all went into the parlor. Standing in front of a mahogany fireplace, Mr. Lowry handed Kevin the keys to his car and tossed Marcia a $10 bill.

"Be sure to take Carole downtown, so she can see what a nice town we live in," he said. "And Kevin, I expect you to show her how Southern gentlemen behave."

"Yes, sir! I will, sir!"

When Kevin opened the door of the red Cadillac convertible with white leather seats, I slid into the front. Marcia tying a tiny pink scarf under her chin, bounced into the back.

"So what year are you in school?" she asked.

"Oh, I'm not going to school right now," I said. "None of us are."

Remembering how Dad had warned us to be careful about telling people we didn't go to school, that if the authorities ever found out, they might take us kids away from him, I was sorry I said anything, so I made up a lie. "Mom's going to enroll us in a Calvert School correspondence course next semester," I said. "It's very exclusive. She saw an ad in National Geographic. Ambassadors send their kids there."

I hadn't been in a car for months and Kevin drove fast, so I gripped the door handle tight. As we sped down wide streets lined with old oak trees and Spanish moss, past the local high school, the downtown area, and the church the Lowrys attended, Kevin and Marcia gossiped about friends and chuckled over inside jokes. I wanted to say something smart and clever, but I couldn't think of anything.

Finally, squealing into a local hamburger joint, Kevin came to a stop. As he gave our order to the carhop, he kept looking at himself in the side mirror. Every now and then one of their male friends would saunter over. Eyes sized me up, and one boy whistled. "Wow! Where'd ya'll find *her*?"

Chuck Berry's "School Days" pumped out of the neon-lit building surrounded by groups of kids and dozens of cars. I began bouncing up and down, shaking my shoulders and snapping my fingers. Nodding his head in approval, Kevin slid over to my side and reached beneath my seat. When he pulled out a silver flask, a rainbow of neon colors flashed across his face. "It's the old man's." He giggled. "He thinks we don't know."

Marcia made a face and stuck her tongue out. "Oh, poor us, Carole." She put her hand to her forehand in a dramatic gesture. "Daddy is a drunk." Then, she let out a shrill laugh.

I wasn't at all happy with the way things were going. Marcia and Kevin kept passing the flask around, and I had a feeling they didn't like me. I was about ready to say I wasn't feeling well, when Kevin slid across the seat again. This time he put his arm around me.

"You ever kiss a nigger, Carole?

For a minute I felt confused. Was Kevin serious or was he just teasing me? I really couldn't tell, but I knew I was dying for a cigarette.

"So where do the hoods hang out?" I asked.

"The hoods?" Marcia chuckled. "What are hoods?"

She tried passing me the flask, but I pushed her hand away.

"You know. The hoods. In my school in Chicago, you were either a collegiate or a hood. The collegiates were on the college track. The hoods or hoodlums were...uh, well, I guess you could call them the bad kids."

Kevin took a big gulp from the flask and held it high in the air. "To the hoods!" he shouted.

Marcia pulled herself forward between the seats and grabbed the flask from Kevin. "Oh, you mean the cruds, Carole!" She wiped her mouth with the back of her hand. "We don't have anything to do with the cruds."

By the time we drove home, Kevin was weaving all over the road, and Marcia was slumped in the back. When we got to the yacht club, I saw Mom and Dad waiting on deck. All I wanted to do was fall into my bunk, but I knew they would expect to hear about my night on the town.

"Great kids, weren't they?" Dad said.

"And so genteel, too!" Mom chimed in. "Milly said Kevin wants to be a jet pilot. They're sending Marcia to law school."

I wanted to tell mom that the Lowrys were not as genteel as she thought and that Marcia and Kevin were mean kids who drank too much, but I didn't want to spoil things for her.

After I gave my parents a brief run-down about the places we'd visited, I went down below. When I climbed into my bunk, Gale raised up on one elbow. "Oh, oh." She said. "I smell alcohol."

"Shhh!" I put my finger across my lips. "It wasn't me. It was those kids."

"Yeah, sure." Gale sneered. "I'm going to tell."

"Don't you dare," I whispered. "If you shut up, I'll let you wear my blue scarf."

"Pinky-swear?" She held her little finger up.

"Sure." I lied. "Now go back to sleep."

As the *Elizabeth* floated downstream toward Vicksburg, Mom and Gale spent most of their time studying books about places we would soon visit. A deep love of history bonded them, and Gale knew almost as much as Mom did about the big plantations on the Natchez Trace.

The further south we traveled, the more humid the air became, so we stayed on deck, wearing as few clothes as possible. Timmy and I spent hours learning to make monkey-fist key chains and figure-eight coasters from white cotton rope. We usually worked in the cockpit, so we could keep Dad company.

Standing at the wheel, he enjoyed entertaining us with our
favorite songs or tales about the fabulous food we'd find in New
Orleans, the white beaches in Florida, or the pineapple
plantations in Cuba. Nothing escaped Dad's eye. Every now and
then, he'd see something interesting, and a lesson about life
would commence.

"Look, a submerged log coming up on our bow. That thing
could damage our propeller if we hit it. You know feelings are
like that. If you shove things down into your subconscious mind,
you won't even know that they're there. Later they'll come up
again and cause problems. It's best to get your feelings out when
they're fresh, even if people don't like it. Whoa! Look at that
crane standing beside that pier! Have you ever seen a bird that
big? "

I loved everything about this time. I loved the way my
father's melodious voice stitched songs and stories together while
I pushed my wooden fid through tight strands of rope, the way
every bend in the river brought us something new--here a half-
sunken wreck, there a shanty-style houseboat. Occasionally a cow
would amble over to the riverbank to gaze at us with a blank
stare.

Sometimes when I played guitar, Mom, Gale, and Tim would join in for a chorus or two. Our family songfests were loud and boisterous, but that was okay. No one was around to hear except ourselves:

> *When I was a student at Casey's,*
> *I played on my Spanish guitar.*
> *I flirted with all the young ladies,*
> *and soon I became a Papa...*

In Vicksburg, we tied up alongside the steamboat *Sprague.* Mom had already told us about her glory days on the river, but nothing could have prepared us for the sight of her. At 276 feet, the *Sprague* was a monster. Dubbed "Big Mama" by the men who worked on her, she could push a string of barges as wide and long as a city block, and hours after she steamed past, the river would still be boiling from her enormous wake.

Unfortunately, by the time we got there, neglect had left the *Sprague* in a sorry state. Most of her plush interior had been gutted, and her hull was scaled with rust. The big wheel on her enormous stern sat silent, but we marveled at its intricate wooden paddles. Eager to stretch our legs, Gale and Timmy and I scampered onto the enormous hulk, enjoying the way our screams and laughter echoed inside her hollow interior.

One afternoon, Mom took us to a battlefield on the edge of the river. Sitting in the trenches, she explained the siege of Vicksburg so vividly we all felt the thirst and hunger of the desperate townsfolk. Tim whipped across the sacred battlefield carrying a tiny Confederate flag, and Gale found a minie-ball half-stuck in the ground.

After Vicksburg, came Natchez. For as long as I could remember, Mom had been fascinated by the dark underworld of crime. Whenever she talked about the shadowy world of lawless renegades, outlaws, and crooks, she smiled the way a kindly mother might when discussing a brood of unruly children. Silver Street in Natchez was notorious for its lawlessness. It could be, she said, one of the big highlights of our trip.

"What a place, kids! Walking along the riverfront, you could see slaves from the Congo carrying baskets on their heads. Tinkling piano music and the laughter of rowdy men spilled from the smoke-filled saloons. Horse's hooves clanged down the street and sometimes there were even gunfights. Natchez-under-the-hill was a dangerous place, but oh, so thrilling! Jim Bowie, the knife guy, got into a big fight out on a sandbar there once. Crowds gathered and bets were made. Poor Jim Bowie got wounded, but not before he'd killed several men. He even disemboweled one while a crowd of blood-thirsty spectators cheered him on. I can hardly wait to walk down that street."

Hours before we arrived in Natchez, we were all dressed and ready to go. As Dad turned the *Elizabeth* around, Mom rushed to the bow. Her eyes scanned the shoreline looking for buildings, but all she saw was a weed-covered path where Silver Street was supposed to be. Only a couple of boarded-up buildings remained of the once-famous place.

Even though Silver Street disappointed Mom, Natchez wasn't a total bust. The bus tours she took to the plantations on the Natchez Trace made up for it. *Longwood, Rosalie, The Briars.* Their strong white columns, formal flower gardens, and slave quarters offered a vivid picture of the way people lived during the Civil War.

"Oh, Lordy!" She said. "I felt just like Scarlett O'Hara!"

By that time, we had all picked up a slight Southern accent. It was impossible not to, if we wanted the local people to understand us, and besides we loved Southern speech. *He slid down that roof quicker than a bee-stung bear on a greased pole. She weren't no bigger than spit.* How could you not want some of that colorful language to come out of your own mouth? At first, we were just playing a role, but eventually, it became perfectly natural.

Living on a boat means you have to share your space. Sometimes I needed to be alone, so I'd wander away from the family. One day, feeling this way, I decided to explore a hill high above our dock. As I climbed the dry sandy path to the top of it, a cool March wind blew my hair back from my face. Far below, the *Elizabeth* looked tiny. Looking north, I could see the river winding its way like a silver ribbon back to Chicago. Looking south, I thought about New Orleans. Dad said we'd be staying there for a while, and I couldn't wait to experience the Crescent City.

The vast landscape at my feet captured my concentration so completely, I startled when I heard the sound of spilling gravel off to my right. When I looked up, I saw a skinny boy about my own age approaching.

"That yur big sailboat yonder?"

"Uh huh."

Wearing dirty green pants, a torn cotton T-shirt, and a haircut obviously not from a barber, he planted himself right in front of me. My eyes darted toward the path I'd climbed, but his generous smile disarmed me.

"I come up here a lot." He grinned. "Purty, ain't it?"

Seeing the Mississippi sparkling below us and the patchwork quilt of farmland nestled along its banks, I had to agree.

"We used to live in Chicago," I said. "We're on our way to New Orleans, then the South Sea Islands. I've come to love this big river. It's faster up North, but down here it's nice and quiet."

The boy's eyes shifted from the sky to his bare feet. "I'm Sam Hoop. I ain't never been further than my Uncle Eddie's place. A two-hour ride."

For a long time we sat on the hill enjoying the sun. Sam had a lot of questions about the boat. He said we must be rich, and that someday he'd like to go some place far away, maybe some place like California.

"Well, I better be gettin' home." Sam sighed.

"Me, too," I said.

Sam stood up and started to go, but then he turned back.

"Hey, you want to go see a movie with me? We got a movie house downtown."

"Sure," I said. "When?"

"How about this Sunday? I usually get the shoes then. Every other. The show starts at five. Paw can take us in his truck."

When I told the family about Sam, Dad said it might not a good idea for me to go off with a total stranger, but Mom leaped up to defend the idea.

"But, Edward. This is Carole's first real date. Don't you think we should celebrate that? I'm sure it'll be okay."

I wanted to protest the word date. In my mind, this was not a real date, just some kid I'd met. A real date would be handsome, someone who'd make me feel like the luckiest girl in the world. Spoiling Mom's excitement seemed mean, though. In spite of having given up all the trappings of a conventional life, I knew deep down she hoped us kids would somehow turn out to be normal.

When Sunday came, Mom brushed and combed my hair. I'd curled it, so it fell in smooth waves to my shoulders. In the tiny head, doing my make-up, I chose dark red lipstick.

"Me too! Me too!" Gale begged. So I poked a few dots on her upturned lips.

After dismissing three or four outfits, I finally chose a black-and-yellow calico skirt with three gathered tiers, a white blouse with ruffles, and blue straw wedgies.

When I emerged from the fo'csle, Mom kissed my cheek. "Oh, Carole, you look so pretty! You really ought to get in a beauty contest. I was a finalist once, but you had to wear an evening gown to go to the next level. My family couldn't afford one."

I was hoping Dad would compliment me, but he never did. He admired the way I'd learned to handle the boat. He thought I was smart; I knew that. But when it came to beauty, mine seemed to escape him.

"Did you put the plank out, Edward? His parents might want to come aboard." The plank Mom was talking about was a ten-foot slab of hardwood wide enough for a person to use as a gangplank.

At five o'clock we all sat in the cockpit. We couldn't see the road at the top of the hill, but eventually we heard the growl of an engine and a squeal of brakes.

Dad stood up. "That must be them."

A few minutes later, Sam scooted down the hill. His too-short black suit jacket left his thick wrists exposed, and it looked like a dog had gnawed the cuffs of his blue jeans, but he did wear shoes, a pair of black loafers that slid off the back of his heels. As he came teetering across the gangplank, a Piggly Wiggly shopping bag thumped against his legs.

After Sam sat down, he rustled around in his bag; then he turned toward Mom.

"This here's a present for you, Ma'am. Maw thought yuh might need it. Wereas yur travelin' and all."

It was a box of commodities, the kind of powdered milk the government gave to poor people, but the way Mom received it with extended hands, it could have been a box of Fannie Mae candies.

"Oh, that was so thoughtful, Sam. Please tell her I said thank you. We don't have a refrigerator on board, so this dry milk will really come in handy."

Sam reached in his bag again. This time he pulled out a floppy bouquet of paper flowers made from pinched-together Kleenex. "These are for you, Carole." He pointed to a few bright slashes of pink on the flowers' ruffled edges. "That's lipstick." He giggled. "My sister Martha makes em."

When Mom heard the sound of the truck engine revving at the top of the hill, she swiveled her head. "Aren't your parents coming down?"

"Naw, it's just my Paw. Maw's sick."

"Well, I'm sorry to hear that." Mom frowned. "Tell her I hope she gets better soon."

Having had enough of formality and good manners, I stood up. Sam stood up too, and then my parents. I wanted to say there was no need to escort us up the hill, but I knew Dad would want to meet Sam's father.

Just before our entourage crested the hill, we heard the truck grind gears, and its motor sputtered. A strong smell of gasoline floated in the air. Walking behind Sam, I noticed his strong neck and wide shoulders. In spite of his clothes and haircut, he looked pretty good from the back.

When we finally reached the road, Dad stopped abruptly, and we all piled against him. Sam's father's truck shook and shuddered at the roadside. A row of lights perched crookedly across the top of its dented cab. Behind it, a round tank with all kinds of black hoses was slowly spinning around. A homemade plywood sign dangled above the rear bumper: *Hoop & Sons Cesspool Cleaning. Your waste is our bread and butter."*

The way Sam lifted his hand to help me climb aboard the belching contraption made me think of Cinderella. Okay, so it wasn't pretty, but that wasn't Sam's fault.

When we got to the movie house, a small knot of kids outside turned to watch Sam's father's truck lurch to the curb.

"Y'all have a good time." Mr. Hoop grinned. "Call me when it's time tuh come and git yuh."

As Sam helped me dismount from the cab, a tall, redheaded girl wearing a thin green dress turned to a friend. "Well, if that don't beat all!"

The movie was *Raintree County*, a story about a young man who changed after he left his hometown. It made me wonder how different things would be if I ever went back to Chicago.

After the movie, Sam's father drove us back to the boat, and Sam insisted on walking me home. As we came to the bottom of the hill, a pink moon spread a rose carpet across the water.

"Thanks for goin' with me," Sam said.

"Thanks for asking."

"I told yuh, I wasn't always goin' to stay here. Someday I'm goin' to go someplace with more jobs."

"You should, Sam. You're smart. And you're awfully nice."

"Shucks, I am not!"

"You are, too."

"But, what are you goin' to do after you git to the islands, Carole? Y'all plannin' on stayin' there?"

"I don't know. Right now, I just hope we make it. It's a long way away."

"You're real purty. You'll probably get married."

"I want to," I said. "I'd like to have someone love me like that."

Before we said goodnight, we stood there a long time, watching small groups of swirling eddies being swept downstream.

We only stayed one night in Baton Rouge. The engine compartment had been collecting water, so every now and then the motor stuttered. "Too much vibration." Dad said. "It's not really a leak, just seepage, but I better take care of it now."

Troweling wet cement around the place where the propeller shaft entered the hull, Dad was pleased. "That ought to fix it," he said.

But the next morning, only a few minutes after getting underway, Mom popped her head out of the companionway hatch. "Stop! Stop!" She sputtered. "There's water all over the place!"

Dad shut the motor off and dropped anchor. Bending over the soaking-wet engine compartment, he shook his head. "When the cement set up, it left a small pocket. Darn! I guess I made the problem worse."

Dad pondered the problem while Mom wiped up the galley.

When he came into the fo'csle to deliver his solution, Gale and I groaned.

"Sorry, but we'll have to pump the water out when we're underway," he said. "I have that small hand pump. You girls can take turns."

"But that means all day." Gale stuck her bottom lip out and twisted her hair.

"No, it doesn't. You can take two-hour shifts. Once we get the mast up, we won't be using the engine. It's just until then."

A few minutes after we were underway again, Dad poked his head through the hatch.

"How's that working, Carole?"

"It's noisy and boring," I shouted.

Mom was starting to make lunch, but Dad asked her to take the wheel a few minutes.

"I don't know, Edward."

"You'll be fine, Marie. There isn't much traffic, and no current, just follow the buoys."

The next thing I knew, Dad was setting a typewriter on my lap, his old metal Royal with green keys. "Write a story about our trip. It'll make the time go by fast. You'll see. The hardest thing in the world to do is write a good sentence."

After he went back on deck, I tried it. Pumping with one hand and typing with other, I started writing an article I thought *Yachting* magazine might like, but after several starts, I gave up. The engine noise made it impossible to think, and, besides, I couldn't come up with even one good sentence. Instead, I asked Mom to bring me a book.

"The Melville one on my bunk," I shouted.

The next thing I knew Gale was tapping me on the shoulder.

Below Baton Rouge, we hit the low, flat lands of the Delta, and the river widened. The sun grew hotter, and our skin darkened. Because piloting wasn't dangerous anymore, and the river was deep enough to not worry about running aground, Dad let me take the wheel often. It pleased me to know how much he depended on me--not just to follow orders, but also to make split-second decisions. I loved the look of shock on people's faces when they saw our big schooner glide by with only a young girl at the wheel.

These were glorious days. After 1,200 miles of river, it seemed time no longer mattered. Two years? Ten? Who cared how long our trip might take? At that point, I would have been content to live aboard the *Elizabeth* for the rest of my life.

As we approached the New Orleans Industrial Canal, Gale and I bounced in and out of the head, primping for our grand entrance. When Mom finished washing the breakfast dishes, she twirled her dishtowel and strutted around the galley. "We'll party hearty here, girls!"

A few minutes later, we heard Dad yell, "Everybody on deck! Quick!"

Thinking it was an emergency, we all clambered up the companionway ladder. "Look over there! I told you!"

Standing on a small jetty of land, we saw our first palm tree. *Hip! Hip! Hooray! Hip! Hip! Hooray!* Barefoot, but all decked out in her antebellum dress, Gale did a little jig across the deck, and Tim ran for the binoculars. When Mom moved beside Dad, he slid his arm around her waist. That's a picture I'll never forget, the two of them standing at the wheel, against a backdrop of clear blue sky, a look of utter bliss on their sunburned faces.

After Baton Rouge, the only sounds we'd heard, other than thumping towboat motors, were nature sounds, the slow slap of water against the hull, the hoot of an owl, and our own voices, but when we approached New Orleans, our ears filled with

incredible music, the hustle and bustle of an international port.
As dozens of small speedboats screamed across our bow, bells,
whistles, and the low moans of sea-going ships raced beside
whirling flocks of laughing gulls. Tim's head swiveled back and
forth, trying to take it all in. His eyes squinted beneath the white
sailor-hat he'd started wearing at a jaunty angle. *Look! Look over
there!*

A four-masted square-rigged training ship from Spain stood
at anchor right off our starboard bow. I'd never seen a more
breathtaking sight. When we came alongside her, the sailors
waving at us from her crow's nest looked as tiny as ants.

As we motored past the downtown area, the bitter smell of
hops brewing in the Jax beer factory mingled with the fragrance
of flower gardens. The smell of Cajun cooking, chicory coffee,
and sweet pralines mingled with the musk of ancient buildings.
As the *Elizabeth* hobby-horsed past the busy port, my mind
raced ahead to the Gulf of Mexico, its turquoise waters waiting to
take us to Florida and beyond.

We spent our first night as guests at the New Orleans Yacht
Club, but Dad knew if we were going to stay awhile, we'd have to
find a permanent dock. A man on a catboat told us where to
look, so the next morning we rounded the rocky jetty by the

coast guard station. Bart's Seafood Restaurant stood at the entrance to the West End Canal. Its rickety, wooden staircase carried a steady stream of customers from a small dock to the upstairs eatery. After Bart's, a two-story industrial building came into view. A couple of platinum blondes on its balcony waved at us from a jungle of tropical plants, and we waved back. *Taylor's Diving & Salvage*.

I shouted. "Holy cow! Look at that!"

In front of the building, a 100-foot schooner with gold-leaf lettering on its transom was tied to a dock. Her name was the *Jesting,* out of New London, Connecticut, and she was the saltiest looking sailboat I'd ever seen. Her long thick bowsprit made the *Elizabeth's* look like a matchstick.

Dad tilted his head to gaze up at her tall masts. "Good God! You could go around the world in that thing, Carole. Just look at the size of those spars!"

As we drew alongside the *Jesting*, a young man, about thirty, wearing a pair of low-slung cut-off shorts stood up and waved. With his bronzed skin and sun-bleached crew cut, he looked like one of those seasoned sailors featured in *National Geographic.* I begged Dad to let me take the wheel.

By the time I'd maneuvered the boat to our new dock in front of Tradewinds, a marine store, the man from the schooner was already there. When Dad handed him our stern line, he winked at me and smiled. "Nice job," he said. After Dad invited the handsome stranger aboard, he held his hand out.

"We're the Goodlanders."

"I'm Ed Taylor, but everybody calls me Hempy."

"That's quite a boat you have there," Dad said.

Hempy smiled. "My partners and I bought her up North. She needed a lot of work, but she's shipshape now. After you get settled, come on by, and I'll give you a tour."

Mom, dazzled by our guest's friendly attitude, offered him some ice tea.

"Never touch the stuff," he cackled. "I'm a beer man, or bourbon and water."

The chemistry between Hempy and Dad was apparent. They both loved boats and talked the same lingo. Gathering around our guest, who had plunked himself down on the steering box in the cockpit, we couldn't get enough of his salty talk.

"Coming down here, we got knocked down off Hatteras. We almost lost her. I'm a herring-choker. Started fishing the Atlantic when I was just a kid. Man, what a bitch that was! When you were gutting the fish, you had to piss on your hands to stop them from freezing. You ever been knocked down, Ed?"

"No, never." Dad sounded apologetic. "Most of my sailing experience has been on the Great Lakes, but I've heard about Cape Hatteras--Graveyard of the Atlantic." Dad looked at Mom. "It's off the North Carolina coast, Marie. It's supposed to be pretty darn scary."

"Rip tides, frequent storms, shifting sandbars, the place is littered with wrecks." Hempy pulled on his beak of a nose, and his sky-blue eyes grew cloudy. "They say more than 700 boats have gone down there."

"Jiminy Cricket!" Tim plunked himself down next to Hempy. He started to lift his hand to stroke his crew cut, but Mom glared at him. A couple of hours later, we were still there, perched in the cockpit, listening to Hempy describe his salty adventures, like he was Jack Sparrow and we were a crew of newly enlisted pirates.

"Someday I want to take the *Jesting* on a long cruise," he said, "but right now our diving business is booming, so we have to stay here. Hard aground in our own coffee grounds, you might say. Hey, I need a beer! Why don't you guys come on over? My partner Jean is cooking up a feast. Fresh-caught flounder with homemade mayonnaise."

From that day on, we were all crazy about our new friend. Over white mugs of coffee in the *Jesting's* varnished galley, we listened to his seemingly endless sea stories. Hempy had been a Navy diver for years, but he'd always wanted to own a schooner, so when he got out of the service, he and his friend Mark Banjovich bought the *Jesting.* They sailed her down to New Orleans, where they met Jean Valz, a veteran of the French Resistance and a piano player, who had a son my age named Gerard. I was enchanted when Hempy introduced us, because the young Frenchman kissed my hand, but when he flipped it over and started swirling his tongue in the cup of my palm, I didn't know how to react. Remembering what Mom had said about different customs, I tried to look like this was something I was familiar with, but when no one was looking, I wiped my hand off on the back of my bathing suit. I seldom got out of my bathing suit, the whole time we lived in the canal. The Louisiana heat made it hard to breathe, so Gale and I were always jumping into the water.

"You shouldn't be swimming in that canal. It's filthy."
Everyone said the canal water would make us sick, but Dad just
laughed it off.

"What are they afraid of? Yeah, I know. It feels kind of
slimy, but it's only silt. Just hose yourself down when you get out."

The handsome, macho crew of divers at Taylor Diving &
Salvage all had nicknames, like Frenchie the Crawfish; Lem the
Bull; and Sam the River Rat. They drove fancy cars and dated
gorgeous women. Someone was always playing the guitar or
concertina, and all of them loved to cook. After so many of
Mom's frugal meals, we relished their gourmet dinners,
everything from jambalaya shrimp to cherries jubilee. After
every meal, Hempy would squint one eye, like Popeye. "I wonder
what the peasants are doing tonight?" he'd say.

Before long I was like a mascot, always hanging around with
Hempy and the divers. Sometimes, in the morning, I would sail
the dinghy down the canal to drink strong chicory coffee and
smoke Picayune cigarettes with the men. I hadn't mastered the
art of sailing my little dinghy in such a narrow canal, so often I
would fly right by the boat.

"Hey, Carole? Where you going?" The men would laugh.

Often, in desperation, I'd just ram the dinghy into one of the *Jesting's* huge ports and clamber aboard pirate-style.

After a while, I got to know Jean Vals' wife Bobbie. They lived in the apartment upstairs of the shop, and Bobbie was everything I ever wanted to be. Movie-star glamorous, with almost-white platinum hair to her waist, she always had a tiny Pomeranian dog tucked under her arm.

"She eats birdseed." Bobbie chucked the little dog under its chin.

Bobby worshipped the sun and had a great tan, so I felt honored when she invited me to join her on on the balcony. She taught me how to mix her secret sun-tanning concoction of mercurochrome and baby oil, and she let me rub her down with it. One night, I saw her all dressed up. She was standing on the balcony, waiting to go with Jean to the Monteleone Hotel where he was playing. Her strapless white gown revealed her brown satin breasts. A choke-collar of diamonds adorned her neck. Red fingernails moved nervously over a circle of light. "I have a little gold chain that goes with it. Jean thinks it's cute for me to be chained to his piano while he plays. People love it!"

The apartment upstairs of the shop was elegant and modern, but not nearly as interesting as the downstairs, a vast, high-ceiling industrial space with a fancy office. Out in front of the building, right beside the steep cement steps that led to the apartment, Lem's mean bulldog stood guard.

"Spike is really a pussycat." Lem hugged the muscular, loose-lipped dog while it licked his hand like a pork chop. "But, if anyone he doesn't know tries to go up those stairs, he'll rip their face off."

Because the dog lunged and pulled on its heavy chain every time I went near it, I avoided the front of the shop. Arriving by dinghy was much easier, anyway. Being on the other side of the canal, if I walked there, I had to go all the way to the end and circle back.

The shop bustled with activity as crews of divers came and went. Most of Hempy's salvage business was done on the offshore oil rigs. Hanging on the walls, heavy canvas deep-sea diving suits looked funny without people in them. When I tried lifting a weighted boot, Hempy laughed. "Thinking about taking up diving?"

"No way, Jose!" I said. "I'd be terrified underwater."

Hempy's brass globe-like diving helmet fascinated me. I tried to imagine what it would be like to be inside it, but when I peeked into the round faceplate with the little cage in front, all I saw was darkness.

Hempy's sleek XK140 Jaguar was his prize possession. It had long curved fenders and a new candy-apple red paint job that you could see your face in.

"Hey, Carole, want to go into town with me?"

Going into town usually meant going to the French Quarter. In the dimly-lighted bars where he was a regular, Hempy sometimes let me take a sip of his bourbon or sneak a swig of beer. Conversation between us was easy. There was always so much to talk about--the trip he was going to take to Cape Canaveral to sign a big contract, waterfront gossip, or the wild goings-on of his crew. Sometimes, the bartenders who didn't know him would think Hempy was my father. They'd say, "Your father ordered you a Coke," or "Do you want me to put this on your father's tab?"

Nose-to-nose in a small booth in the back of the bar, we giggled about that. Knocking a cold bottle of Heineken beer against my shoulder, Hempy would say, "You're only as old as who you feel!"

After we'd been hanging out together a few months, Hempy asked if I wanted to have dinner with him in his pad in the French Quarter.

"Alone?" I asked.

"Sure, I'll whip us up some steaks, and we'll eat on the balcony. It's on Chartres Street right across from the Ursuline convent. They say vampires used to live in its attic. It's a great place to people watch."

When I tried to picture Hempy and me alone in his apartment, I felt a little wary.

"Well, I'll have to ask Dad first."

I was sure my father would say no, but he didn't seem at all concerned.

"Sure, Carole. Why not? You two seem to have fun together."

Mom pressed for more details.

"What? Hempy has a pad in the French Quarter? Where? He wants to cook dinner for you? Gee, I wish I could go. I hear those apartments are gorgeous."

"But it would be just him and me. Usually there are other people around. I'm not sure I want to go."

Dad frowned. "What are you trying to imply, Carole?" Are you trying to say that you think Hempy might be romantically interested in you?"

"Uh huh. He might be. Otherwise, why didn't he invite the whole family?"

Dad snickered and Mom rolled her eyes.

"Who knows? But the idea that Hempy might be interested in you that way is ridiculous. You've seen the kind of women that hang around Taylor's. What would he want with a skinny kid like you?"

Hey wait a minute! I thought. *A skinny kid like me?*

"Well, I don't think I'll go," I said. "I thought you guys would say no."

Dad shrugged. "Teenagers," he said.

"Hormones," Mom replied.

Furious that my parents were making fun of me, I decided to change my mind.

"Okay. I will go," I said, "but if anything bad happens, it's not going to be my fault."

Hempy's pad looked like a Humphrey Bogart movie. His second-floor studio had overhead fans, ceramic tile floors, arched doorways, and potted palms. When he opened the tall, louvered doors that led onto the tiny balcony, I heard voices in the street below and the sound of a jazz band in the distance. Peering over the rail, I noticed a couple in front of the convent. The guy had his back against its gray wall. The woman's skirt was hiked up, and one of her legs was wrapped around him. The tall glass that dangled from her hand dribbled a pink stream onto the sidewalk.

"Well, I better get the steaks started." Hempy slid his hand down my arm. "I'll call you when they're ready. In the meantime, feel free to put a record on. The hi-fi is on the bookcase beside the couch."

Listening to Julie London's husky voice, I watched Hempy move around the small kitchen nook. Instead of his usual shorts, he'd put on a pair of blue dress pants and a silky-looking blue shirt. He seemed different dressed like that, smooth and handsome.

The steaks were tender and juicy and the wine a special vintage. As I watched Hempy pour it into a large round glass, I noticed the way the frizzy hairs on his wrist curled around his gold watch.

"Over the lips and over the gums, lookout stomach, here it comes!"

The wine flowed freely and conversation was easy. After we finished eating, Hempy took me by the hand and led me to the couch.

"A little more wine, my dear?" He slid his arm around my waist and chuckled.

"No, I think I've already had too much." I giggled.

I was slumped against end of the couch when he moved closer.

Baby...baby...baby...

As Hempy slid his fingers under my hair, he pressed his nose against my neck. His lips planted a necklace of kisses along my collarbone. When he cupped my breasts in his hands, I knew I should move away, but mystical, keyless doors inside me were opening. I felt warm. I felt receptive.

The next morning Mom cornered me.

"Well? Was it fun?"

"Yes, it was."

I hoped my smile looked normal, not smirky.

"So what was the apartment like? What did you eat?"

I only gave her a few details. I didn't feel ashamed about having sex with Hempy. Hadn't Dad told us natives in the islands had no inhibitions, that if they wanted to make love, they just jumped behind a bush and did it? One time he horrified me by telling me that fathers in certain tribes in Africa introduced their own daughters to sex; that way the caring parent could be sure it was a gentle experience. Ick! Way more than I wanted to know. Dad was always saying people in the United States were prudes. Well, we weren't most people. Certainly not prudes! We were adventurers in search of paradise. Fearless risk-takers. About-to-be South Sea Islanders. The fact that I had been initiated into the mysterious realm of sex by a rich, handsome, boat-crazy guy made me feel lucky, not guilty.

I knew, of course, if Mom and Dad found out, they would have a fit, but they didn't suspect a thing. The only problem with the whole situation was the fact that, once we had sex, Hempy wanted it all the time. I didn't. I liked the hugging and kissing part. Having Hempy's arms around me, knowing I could make him happy, that excited me. But something wasn't right. All the love feelings I had seemed to disappear the minute we took our clothes off. I had heard the term "frigid woman" tossed around, and I knew that was not a nice thing to be. Was I frigid? Was Hempy an oversexed pervert? I had no idea how often normal people did it, so I went to the library to look it up. Three or four times a week! How could that be possible? Mom and Dad's bunk was only about fifteen feet away from ours. If they did it that often, wouldn't I have heard something? For the next few nights, I stayed awake as long as I could, but I heard nothing. Did that mean my parents were abnormal too? Depressed and feeling somewhat responsible for the situation, I sulked.

Back in Chicago, when boys first started showing an interest in me, Dad had warned me. I was in a field beside the boatyard, wrestling with Peter Dreyfus, a boy from school, and Dad happened to walk by. When he saw us rolling around in the dirt, he was livid. Dragging me home by the arm, he told me, in no uncertain terms that wresting with boys was dangerous. "What were you thinking? Letting him get on top of you like that? What the hell were you thinking?"

Dad said getting a reputation for being a prick-tease was the worst thing that could happen to a girl. "Blue balls," he said. "If a male gets aroused too much and has no release, his balls blow up like balloons. They turn blue and get hard as rocks. It's excruciating, Carole. Worse than anything you could ever imagine."

Well, I certainly didn't want to hurt Hempy like that, so I continued to have sex with him, but in order to cool things down, I stopped going over to Taylor's all the time. Instead I took the bus into the French Quarter so I could hang out with the artists in Jackson square. One day an artist in Pirate's Alley asked if he could paint my portrait. "It's called a shill. It's better for business," he said. "If people think I have a customer, they'll stop to watch me work, maybe buy." After other artists heard I was available, I was busy all the time. Soon, dozens of portraits of me were taped to the shelf above my bunk.

Hempy said I was driving him crazy. "Why are you spending so much time in the Quarter? What are you doing down there? I hardly ever see you anymore."

 "I'm not doing anything. If we're together all the time my parents are bound to get suspicious," I said. "This whole thing is making me nervous; eventually they'll put two and two together, and then what?"

"Then, we'll tell them."

Just the thought made my stomach flip over.

"My father will be furious, Hempy."

"No, he won't. Ed and I are friends. I'll make him understand. I'm serious about you, Carole. I want to marry you."

Marry me? *Wow! That **was** serious.* "No! Please!" I begged. "Let's wait. I can't face telling them yet."

"Well, okay," Hempy said. "But I'm crazy about you. You better not be fooling around with anyone else. You're my girl. Aren't you? Just my girl?"

A few weeks later, Mom told us a reporter from the *Times-Picayune* newspaper wanted to write an article about us. His name was Dawson Gordon III and he was totally captivated by our story. Getting down on one knee, he spent a long time snapping pictures of me. "Your family is amazing, Carole," he said. "You're all so free. I can't even imagine growing up in a family like yours. For me, it's always been boarding schools and perfect manners. Compared to yours, my life has been terribly boring."

Before he left, Dawson asked me for a date. I knew Hempy would be mad if I said yes, but I was beginning to wonder if the whole Hempy thing was wrong for me.

Dawson was a perfect gentleman. We went to a juke joint on the edge of town with three of his friends. I danced all night and enjoyed kissing him, but after his article came out with the headline *The Goodlanders Make Huckleberry Finn Look like the Man in the Grey Flannel Suit,* Mom took to her bunk sobbing for three days, and Dawson was no longer welcome aboard the *Elizabeth.*

When Hempy heard I'd gone on a date, he was furious. "I don't want you going out with other guys. Let's tell your parents right now."

"No! Please!" I begged. "Dawson is just a friend. Can't I even have friends?"

"Sure, you can, Lollipop," Hempy said.

Every time Hempy called me Lollipop I cringed. Visions of some kid holding a sucker to his tongue drooled through my mind. Why not just advertise?

"I don't like it when you get mad," I said.

Another friend I had was Randy Rogero, a handsome marine biologist who was totally crazy about me. He had black wavy hair and a deep tan from being outside all the time. He only wore white clothes, which I thought was cool. Randy kept his sleek, varnished speed boat in Tradewinds' backyard. One the best things about being docked in front of the marine store was the cookouts they held every weekend. Crabs, crawfish, shrimp, hushpuppies, and cornbread, the red-checkered, oilcloth-covered picnic tables groaned with food, and gallons of sweet tea were served alongside washtubs of beer. Boatmen from all over came to the canal-side cookouts, and Randy, a local hero, entertained them with hair-raising stories of near misses and speed.

"I don't understand why you're so mean to Randy," Mom said. "He's always stopping by here to see if you're home. You make dates with him, but then you break them. What's going on? A guy like Randy doesn't come along often."

There were other live-aboards in the West End Canal. Jack Kelly, for instance, owned the small power boat in front of ours. A quiet Irishman with black, curly hair and sad eyes, he scraped out a living doing odd jobs. Dusty, his tail-wagging black cocker spaniel lighted up Jimmy's life. One day when our neighbor went into town to estimate a job, he tied Dusty to a stanchion on the stern of his boat. When he came back, he found the poor thing dangling over the side. The little dog felt so lonesome, he'd tried to jump from the boat to the shore. It was a horrible day, and the whole canal felt deeply touched by the tragedy. When I crept to the bow to sneak a smoke that night, I heard Jack sobbing like he was a little kid. It made me cry, too.

Another interesting person was The Bird Girl. Her real name was Robin, but Mom called her The Bird Girl because of the way her short-cropped, black hair stuck up in the back like a crest and the way she liked to stand like a crane on one leg as she sculled her old wooden scow through the oily swamp behind Tradewinds.

The Bird Girl lived with her father aboard a Chesapeake Bay skipjack. Howard had big bushy eyebrows and shifty eyes. He never said much, but Gale liked him. My sister was thrilled to have a best friend, so the two girls spent every day fishing or swimming in the canal. Later, we found out the Bird Girl's father had kidnapped her during a stormy divorce. Gale apparently knew they were on the lam, but she never said a word until after they'd already left for Cuba.

One hot August night, Hempy joined us for dinner. Afterwards we were all going to play *Sorry!,* so Dad brought the game out, but Hempy, sitting on the steps of the companionway ladder, said he had something to say first.

Tim and Gale were choosing their game pieces, and Dad was stacking the cards when Hempy began.

"Ed and Marie," he said, "you know how much your friendship means to me, your whole family. I've wanted to say something, but I had to be sure. Carole and I are in love. I'm asking permission to marry your daughter."

Dad's head jerked up from the game board. His eyebrows arched, and one knee was pumping up and down. "What did you say?"

Hempy looked sheepish. "I'm asking your permission to marry Carole."

Dad groaned. "Oh, Jesus, Hempy! How could you? We trusted you with our daughter."

For a long time all I could hear was the sound of water lapping against the *Elizabeth's* hull, but then Mom started talking, and, man, was she angry. Putting both hands on her hips, she said, "Carole is only 16, Hempy! She's vulnerable, and you took advantage of that. Shame on you! Carole's not ready to marry anybody."

"I don't think you people give her enough credit," Hempy persisted. "I'm not saying we have to get married right away. I mean, we'll get engaged first. Then, maybe in a year or two...."

Dad's eyes looked like BB shots. "So what do you have to say, Carole? Do you love Hempy? Do really want to marry him?"

Sitting there, suddenly feeling sick, I almost backed out, but then I saw the soft, confident grin on Hempy's face, and my heart melted. How could I not want to marry a man like that, a man who loved me so much? Someone who could offer a life of fun and adventure on the water? I could already see the honeymoon picture: Hempy and me on the *Jesting* sailing toward a rose-colored horizon. Moving beside him, I put my hand on Hempy's knee. "I do," I said. "We love each other. I want to marry Hempy."

Dad grabbed Mom by the elbow. "We need to talk about this, Marie."

As the two of them disappeared into the main cabin, I started to cry, but Hempy wrapped his arms around me.

"Don't worry, baby," he said. "It will be okay. I promise."

Gale bounced her green game piece up and down in her palm. "I knew it!" she said.

Tim didn't look at me. He just kept spinning his blue man around and around on the table.

Dad hardly ever raised his voice, but that night he was almost bellowing. In between outbursts, Mom's softer voice rose and fell.

When they finally came back into the galley, Mom was wiping her eyes. Dad seemed calmer, but I knew he was still upset because he let Mom do the talking.

"Well, Hempy," she said, "I guess there's nothing we can do about this now. Carole's too young to know what she wants, and you should have known better, but if you love her, and she thinks she loves you, then I guess you can be engaged."

"You know she'll change her mind," Dad said. "You know we'll be leaving New Orleans soon. She'll have to be eighteen before you can marry her."

After she saw how embarrassed Hempy looked, Mom softened. "We'll let you know where we are," she said. "We're going to Pensacola next. It's not that far by car. We've always liked you, Hempy. You know that."

"Thanks, Marie. You won't be sorry," Hempy said. "She'll never want for anything."

Later in my bunk, I mulled over my parents' reactions. Somehow I had expected more of a fight, for Dad to punch Hempy in the nose maybe or shoot him with the spear gun that hung on the tool room wall. In the square of the hatch above me, I saw a small twinkling star. It reminded me how the sky looked when we were on the river far away from any light. Vast space, millions of visible stars, and countless ones behind them. Rolling over to hug my pillow, I fell asleep.

Hempy gave me my diamond ring on the patio of the Court of Two Sisters Restaurant. We held hands all through dinner and talked about our future. When it came time for dessert, the waiter slid a white china plate in front of me. Then he carefully placed a tiny blue velvet box in the center of it.

"Go ahead, Lollipop, open it!"

When I snapped the lid open, the big diamond with two smaller ones on each side sparkled with light.

"Oh! Gee, Hempy. It's beautiful! "

When he slid the engagement ring on my finger, I felt like running from table to table to show everyone. All the doubts I'd suffered melted away. Hempy was my love, my husband to be. Forget about the sex problem. Surely that was something I'd grow into. It didn't seem to matter anyway. When Hempy asked, so sweetly, "Was it good for you, baby?" I always said yes.

A couple weeks later, walking back from the yacht club where I'd gone to retrieve our forwarded mail, I was so busy reading a letter from Mickey. I almost bumped into a burly man sitting on a red Harley at a stop sign.

"Oops, sorry!" I waved the letter at him. "Good news. I wasn't paying attention."

When the man, wearing blue jeans and a red-and-white flowered Hawaiian shirt, twisted around to adjust the feet of a small green parrot perched on his shoulder, his wide brimmed, palm-frond hat rattled loudly.

"Aren't you the girl from that schooner at Tradewinds?" Stubby fingers pulled through a full brown beard. "My name's

Walter Kupik. I've been meaning to get over there to meet you folks, but I've been busy working on my own boat, a Tarpon Springs sponge boat. I'm getting her ready for a long sea voyage. In a few months, I'll be heading for Tahiti."

Que cuerva! Que cuerva! The parrot let out a long scream, followed by a sexy wolf-whistle.

"It means 'what curves' in Spanish." Walter patted the parrot's head. "I got him in Belize last year."

"Tahiti? That's in the South Seas, right? We might be going there! You've got to meet my parents. Come home with me now. They'll be so thrilled!"

Walter's eyes lighted up at my bubbling enthusiasm. "Hop on," he said, gesturing toward the Harley. After he tucked the parrot inside his shirt, I flipped my leg over the bike, and off we went.

My parents almost fell over when they heard Walter had sailed three times to Tahiti.

"Imagine that!" Mom gushed.

Mom and Dad asked Walter a million questions. What was it like? Where was the best place to dock? Was it expensive?

"Everything they say about it is true." Tears welled up in Walter's eyes. He put his hand on his heart. "It's Paradise on earth, and the natives are beautiful. Not just the women either. Why do you think so many ancient sailors used to jump ship when they got there? The Tahitians have nothing to do all day but party and fish. When sailors used to stop in Tahiti to provision their ships, the women would row out in canoes to welcome them. All those guys had to do was choose the one they wanted. When the ships left, the *wahines* would go down to the beach to see them off. They'd beat their chests and weep and moan, but the minute the ship's masts disappeared over the horizon, they'd throw a big party and wait for the next ship."

"Gee," Mom said. "Those guys had it made. How long are you staying, Walter?"

"Legally you can only stay six months." Walter sighed. "It's a thousand mile trip, beating against the wind to sail to someplace that will renew your visa. This time, I'm not coming back though. Life in the States? Man, it's a bughouse here. I have a friend who has a house in the mountains. She'll hide me."

After awhile, I got tired of listening to the boat talk so I walked over to West End Park. Sitting cross-legged on the grass there, I finished reading Mickey's letter. Apparently he was planning a visit, but he didn't know where the boat would be docked.

By the time I got back, Walter was gone, but Mom said we were going to his house that night for dinner.

"He owns an apartment building in the Quarter," she said. "He offered to let us take hot showers. Being a sailor, he knew, of course, how much we'd enjoy that. He's such a character, Carole!"

As we strolled through the Quarter to Walter's house, the sound of clanking dishes and the smell of stale beer spilled onto Royal Street. Strip-joint hawkers shouted at tourists streaming past their dingy clubs. Every time a door opened, Dixieland jazz, loud bongos, or Beat poets spouting verses spilled into the street. When Tim lingered too long in front of a poster displaying pictures of a stripper named Chesty Morgan, Mom grabbed his hand and yanked him forward.

"912 Toulouse," Dad said. "This is it."

In the shadowy corridor that ran alongside the ancient stucco building, Mom grabbed my arm and squeezed it. "If only these walls could talk," she whispered.

The small dark patio behind the house had a wrought iron balcony. Potted palms stood like sentries between four upstairs apartments.

Timmy ran to a tall banana tree in the center of the courtyard. "Look, real bananas!"

On the back wall someone had hung a dugout canoe and a row of wooden masks. When we came to a Dutch door at the back of the house, we saw Walter standing in front of a big black steel stove. He was bare chested, with only a blue-and-white flowered sarong slung across his hips. His parrot, perched on a stand in the kitchen, flapped its wings. *Que cuerva! Que cuerva!*

"Welcome, farmers!" Walter chuckled at his own irony. After he wiped his hands on a kitchen towel, he led us to a front room where a woman in a pale yellow dress played a white upright piano.

"This is my wife, Iona."

Big brown eyes twinkled beneath a head of tousled grey curls. Waving one hand while she kept playing with the other, Iona threw her head back and shouted, "Welcome to 912 Toulouse!" After the song was over, Walter's petite wife stood up. She extended her hands and pulled each one of us against her rose-scented body. For such a tiny woman, she sure had strong arms.

Walter swept his hand toward a sofa and a couple of chairs. "Have a seat," he said. "Who wants a beer?"

After a few minutes of chit-chat, Walter returned to the kitchen, and Iona resumed her piano playing. Mom really dug the music. It didn't take long before her feet were tapping the tile floor. Dad's head started jerking back and forth like a chicken.

When Iona finally asked if we were ready to take a shower, Gale jumped up. "Me first! Can I be first?"

"Come with me." Iona smiled. "I'll show you where everything is."

After we followed her to the bathroom, she pulled a stack of thick white towels from a tall black cabinet with Oriental designs. A few minutes later Walter, carrying a stack of colorful-looking fabrics, joined us.

"Here," Walter said, "these are *pareaus*. My Tahitian friend Michelle prints them and sells them at the flea market. They're totally authentic. If you plan to visit Tahiti, you better learn how to wear one."

Mom giggled. "Are we supposed to put these on now?"

"Sure," Walter said. "Unless you'd rather be naked?"

After Mom chose a red-and-white one, Walter crooked his finger at Gale.

"Come here," he said. "I'll demonstrate how to tie them. The *wahines* have dozens of ways to wear these things, but mostly they sling them around their hips and go bare-breasted. You guys are too square for that, so just tie the ends around your neck like this."

After each of us, wearing our bright pareaus, came back from our bath, we twirled in front of Walter and Iona.

"Beautiful! Gorgeous! Hubba-hubba!" Iona gushed.

None of us had ever seen Dad in a skirt before, so when he came out, we all started giggling.

"I really like how this feels." Dad slid his palms along the soft colorful fabric. "So much more comfortable than pants."

Walter served dinner at a long mahogany table big enough to seat twenty people. In the background, a chorus of fierce chanting voices and loud drums could be heard. "You guys should have been here last night." Walter broke off large chunks of bread from a crusty loaf on a wooden board. "Zsa Zsa was here with her whole entourage."

"Gabor?" Mom gasped. "She was here?"

"Have you ever met Elvis Presley, Walter?" Gale asked hopefully.

"Sure. During the filming of *King Creole* he used to hang with us a lot. He sat right where you're sitting. We call that the Elvis chair."

While we were feasting on his gourmet dinner, Walter told us he was only fifteen when he first went to sea as a cabin boy on a German freighter. By the time he was twenty, he'd rounded the Cape of Good Hope three times. On her teaching salary, Iona didn't have enough money to travel by ocean liner, so that's how they met.

"It was love at first sight," she said. "Walter looked like a Greek God." Tapping her slim fingertips on her husband's big belly, Iona chuckled. "Now he looks like the Buddha."

When they were young, Walter and Iona owned several boats. They lived aboard them and sailed all over Cuba, Mexico, the Virgin Islands, Costa Rica and Venezuela.

"How did you like Tahiti, Iona?" Mom asked.

"Oh, I've never been there." Iona's long eyelashes flashed like butterflies when she blinked. "It takes months to get to Tahiti. I have my teaching job to think about, and someone has to stay here to look after the apartments."

After a few weeks of hanging out with Walter, Dad started wearing his *pareau* around the boat. He tossed his worn leather Topsiders overboard and bought a pair of sandals.

When Walter found out we didn't have a horn, he presented Dad with a pink and white conch shell. "It doesn't take batteries," Walter said. "It's louder than most regular horns, anyway. Conches are the only horns sailors use in the islands. This one came from a market in Papeete, Tahiti's capitol city. "

Sitting on the dock beside the *Elizabeth,* we all took turns trying to blow it. Dad got the hang of it right away. A loud sound, almost like an ocean liner horn, blasted across the canal, but when I tried it, the shell just sputtered. After I adjusted my lips, I tried it again, but this time it only farted.

"Here." I passed it over to Gale. "You try."

Gale's blast was clear and pure, but Mom had no luck at all. After a few attempts Tim got a nice clear sound. Rubbing his fingers over his mouth, he frowned. "It makes my lips tickle."

Dad ran his fingers lovingly over the shell's pink rim. "Hey, this will be great for calling you kids. It can be our emergency signal. Three blasts. When you hear me blow that, come back to the boat right away."

All Walter's tenants were colorful characters, artists and entertainers and locals down on their luck. He liked taking care of people. His rents were low and his tenants could always count on a home-cooked meal served with Walter's wise and witty observations about the human race.

Albert Godchaux, a young philosophy student from Montreal, Canada, was my favorite. Albert always dressed in black. He had a scraggly little goatee that he pulled on when he got excited. Because he enjoyed talking about politics and poor people's needs, I thought I could learn a lot, if I hung out with him. Albert had sad beagle-dog eyes, but inside he was a happy man.

Leslie, a tall, blonde ballet dancer, was Walter's constant companion. Leslie always had a faint smile on her face. Her throaty Marlene Dietrich voice and grey eyes intrigued me, so I tried getting to know her better, but Leslie hardly ever spoke. Sprawled like a cat on the living room sofa, she was usually sleeping.

The occupants in Apartment No. 4 were night creatures who never woke before noon. The first time I met Bella and Candy, it was almost three in the morning. They wore strapless sequined dresses, and their tousled platinum curls and huge breasts bounced when they came onto the patio. Obviously, a little drunk, Bella flopped down in a chair, but Candy made a big fuss over me. "Walter! Really! You have to stop hiding these new beauties you find!"

After Bella took off her spike heels, she held her legs out straight.

"They're getting fat, aren't they, Walter? Tell me the truth. My whole routine was off tonight. I danced like a cow."

Candy rolled her eyes. "You're smashed, dear," she said. "Your routine went fine. It's time for bed now."

As I watched the two of them teeter off on their silver, high heel shoes, I felt hot with envy. "They're so beautiful, Walter!"

"They're men," Walter said. "Female impersonators. They work at the My-O-My Club in the West End. It's not far from your boat. I'll take you guys there sometime. "

Mom quickly made Iona her best friend. The two women shared stories about living aboard boats, and sometimes Mom visited Iona in her own studio apartment in the Garden District. Mom said Iona was the most independent woman she had ever met. In spite of the fact that everyone knew Walter and Leslie were lovers, Iona and Leslie were good friends.

"Man," Mom said, "these people sure are broadminded. I never heard of a married couple having separate apartments. I suppose Iona doesn't care because she has all those handsome male students hanging around. They practically live in her studio."

Walter knew Hempy. He knew everyone on the waterfront, but he didn't like my fiancé a whole lot. "What do you want him for? He's way too old for you. If you like the guy, go ahead and screw him, but why get married?"

During the time Dad was making final plans to leave New Orleans, the heat became oppressive. Not a breath of air stirred, and Mom and Dad were going through changes. Usually all bubbly and happy, Mom suddenly grew serious and quiet. She also complained a lot, which was something she had never done before. "Can't you build us an ice-box, Edward? Other boats have them." She was pleased when Dad got a new propane stove, but even that made the galley insufferably hot. "I can't take this heat," she said. Most afternoons, when Dad was walking the docks, talking to other boatmen, or painting signs, Mom climbed into her bunk with a huge window fan blowing right on her. Sometimes, in order to beat the heat, she took a trolley out to Iona's place. Dad wasn't used to Mom tromping all over town alone, so he wasn't too happy about that.

"But Iona has air conditioning," Mom said. "Fans aren't enough in this heat. Besides she's a very interesting woman, Edward. She's a marvelous teacher, and she's been everywhere."

"Well, I think it's wrong for her to be so friendly with her male students."

"Oh, but, it is perfectly okay for Walter to have a girlfriend!

As the long hot summer progressed, everything bothered Mom. Then to make matters worse, Gale suddenly blossomed into a teenager. Mom was used to telling my sister everything, but that summer Gale pretty much abandoned her. When she wasn't primping in the head, she strolled around the waterfront, usually followed by boys. She'd even started keeping a diary, a pink one with a grey poodle on the front and a gold clasp. One day, Walter shocked me by saying, "You're pretty, Carole, but you're square. You'll probably end up being a housewife in suburbia. Your sister is the one who interests me. Gale smolders in a hip kind of way."

One afternoon, when we kids went to see a movie across town, my parents got in an argument. When we came back to the boat, it was almost dark, and Dad was pacing up and down the deck.

"What's the matter?" I asked.

Dad's forehead glistened with sweat, and his eyes looked like a trapped animal's eyes. "Your mother ran away!" he said. "We had an argument. It was silly, really. I walked out, but just for a minute. When I got back she was gone."

"Ran away?" Tim looked worried.

"She probably went to the library," Gale said. "She goes there a lot to get out of the heat."

Dad pulled on his bottom lip. "No. It closes at five."

Gale plopped down in the cockpit. "What makes you think she ran away? Did she take all her stuff?"

When Dad jumped up to run below, we all followed. When he threw open their hanging locker, he groaned. "I knew it! All her clothes are gone!" Next, he searched the head. "Her make-up bag is gone!" He wailed. "Everything she owns is gone!"

Gale looked shocked, and Tim started crying.

"Maybe you should call Iona," I said.

We were still in the process of figuring out what to do when we heard footsteps on deck. The hatch slid open, and Walter came shuffling down the ladder. "Hey, man, you guys look weird. What's happening?"

"Marie ran way," Dad said.

"Ran away where? When? "

"Hell, I don't know!" There were tears in Dad's eyes. "She took everything she owns."

Walter put his wrists backwards on his hips and shook his head. "Man, you guys are crazy. I just saw her at Iona's. All she had was one shopping bag. If that was everything that woman owns, no wonder she ran away."

When Mom came home a few hours later, Dad tried to act cool. "So where were you?" he asked.

Mom frowned. "I was at Iona's. I was going to spend the night, but I changed my mind. Walter called. He said you were having some kind of breakdown. Gee, can't a woman spend a few hours away from her family without everyone falling apart?"

The next morning Gale couldn't resist.

"He thought you were going to run away," she said. "You know, like..."

"Hush up!" I hissed, but Gale didn't stop.

"He was crying," she said.

Mom tossed her a patient smile. "Well, I didn't mean to upset him, but your father is way too uptight. Look at Iona. She does her own thing. Your father has a double-standard when it comes to women."

Before Walter left for Tahiti, he tied his boat next to ours, and it was fun helping him prepare the *Endymion* for her long voyage. Mom took copious notes about what kind of food he bought. Dad asked about things like fresh water and gasoline. The problem with all this closeness, though, turned out to be cock-a-roaches. Walter's boat was crawling with some hardy species he'd picked up the year before in Belize, so pretty soon we were infested too.

'There are cockawoches in my cwayons!" Tim groaned.

"Call the Orkin man!" Mom yelled.

Because Dad believed exterminators were a rip-off, he tried conquering the bugs with insect bombs and sticky traps, but without much luck. Mom, in the meantime, got more and more frustrated. One night I woke to find her sitting in the dark at the dinette table. She had a rolled-up newspaper in one hand and wore a floppy hat. "Don't turn the lights on!" She snarled. "I'm not ready yet. The minute the light comes on they scramble. I can't kill them all, but at least I get some. Each roach can make a million babies." A few minutes later, when we did flick the light on, I saw roaches everywhere. Running for cover, they scampered into every crack and crevice they could find. *Bam! Bam! Bam!* The look on Mom's face was frightening.

As the summer drew to a close, everyone in the family, except me, seemed edgy. Now that I was engaged, Mom and Dad treated me like a grown-up. Hempy and I spent all our spare time openly together, and my artist friends were teaching me to draw portraits.

Francis Whitbeck one of Pirate Alley's best artists said, "You're very good."

"That's my dream!" I said. "I want to be an artist."

"You already are." She smiled. "But, I don't know if that's good or bad."

One night, when they thought everyone was asleep, I heard Mom and Dad talking about me and Hempy.

"Do you think they're having sex?" Mom asked.

"Of course they are, Marie."

"Then we'd better get her out of here, Edward. What if she gets pregnant?"

"Perish the thought!" Dad groaned. "But you're right, Marie. It's time we left New Orleans."

Because sludge from the river, along with seaweed and barnacles from the brackish water in New Orleans, had collected on her bottom, Dad said the *Elizabeth* had to be hauled out before we could head for Florida.

"It'll take the rest of our savings, but it needs to be done."

Young's Boat Yard was located in the swampy area behind Tradewinds. The day we were taking the boat over there, Dad tried to get the motor going, but the old Ford truck engine he'd installed wouldn't start. "That's okay," he said. "We can use the dinghy to tow her." After he lashed the dinghy to the *Elizabeth's* port side, he ordered me into it. "I'll be able to steer her with the wheel," he said. "You just make sure she's got some way on."

It took us a long time to get to the inlet that led to the boatyard because controlling the boat wasn't easy. The *Elizabeth* kept drifting from one side of the canal to the other, but Dad kept waving me on. We were almost ready to make our turn when a 40-foot Chris-Craft cruiser with a high fishing tower came roaring up alongside us.

"Need any help?" the man shouted.

"No," Dad yelled back. "We're fine. We're only going over to Young's."

"Well, it'll be much easier if I tow you. Toss me a line."

I could tell Dad was reluctant, but in the end he gave in.

"Oh, all right, thanks." He ran forward to throw the guy a rope. "But whatever you do, don't go too fast."

The minute the tow rope was fastened, however, it snapped tight, and the *Elizabeth* shot forward, pulling me and the dinghy along with her.

"Hey! Slow down!" Dad yelled. "Slow down!" But his voice was lost in the roar of the powerboat's twin diesels.

As we drew alongside the boatyard dock, Dad waved his arms and jumped up and down. "Stop!" he screamed. "You're going to damn fast! Stop!"

The man in the Chris-Craft turned off his motors, but the momentum kept the *Elizabeth* sliding forward. Dad was still gesturing wildly, as her bowsprit headed directly for the pilothouse of the other boat.

Dad shouted, "Cast off, Carole!" So, I unhooked the dinghy.

When I saw there was going to be a collision, I closed my eyes, but the crunching sound of splintering wood and shattering glass quickly made me open them again. The *Elizabeth's* bowsprit had slid into the high cabin of the cruiser, and the fishing tower leaned across its after-deck like a mangled Erector set toy. Racing to the stern of his boat, the owner of the wounded vessel shook his fist at Dad, but my father waved him off like a mosquito. As I brought the dinghy back alongside, he shot me a dark look.

"Goddamn farmers!" He muttered.

As we headed once again to the boatyard dock, the Chris-Craft swung around. In a puff of diesel fumes, she headed out of the inlet back into the canal.

After we tied the boat up, Dad and I went forward to see if there was any damage, but the *Elizabeth's* bowsprit was stout and intact. Only a brown smear where she had gone through the pilothouse and a few scrapes were visible.

"What an idiot," Dad said. "Those stinkpotters think boats are like cars. They think they can stop on a dime. It's a darn good thing you didn't get hurt."

I was busy helping Dad adjust the car tires we used as fenders when I saw the Chris-Craft owner stalking through the boatyard. His head was bent low, but he had one arm raised over his head, and he was waving a bunch of papers at us. "You almost sunk my boat!" the man bellowed. "Get your insurance papers out!"

"Insurance papers?" Dad tossed him a nasty smile. "A good boatman doesn't need insurance. Besides, this was your fault. You were going way too fast. I warned you. Lucky for us our bowsprit is made of oak. Lucky for you, there's not much damage."

"I'll sue! I'm going to sue you for everything your worth!" the man sputtered.

"Sue away!" Dad sneered. "I have no worth. You're the one that caused all the damage. I told you to go slow!"

It only took one quick glance at the *Elizabeth* for the man to see we were poor, so he stomped off. But not before he let loose a long string of colorful words.

"Hey, watch your language!" Dad nodded his head toward me. "There's a young lady here."

Me swabbing the deck.

Chapter Six

THE DAY WE LEFT New Orleans, a shadow of sadness hung over me, but magical things happen when you're on a boat sailing away from land. As soon as I saw the shoreline diminish and the horizon spread before me, I felt free and happy. Standing on the end of the bowsprit, I remembered what Walter had said about the Tahitian *wahines*. Sure, I would miss Hempy and all the friends I made in the French Quarter, but the good thing about being a sailor was the fact that there would always be another exciting port waiting just beyond the horizon.

It took us awhile to get to the Gulf of Mexico, but when we did, its brilliant turquoise blue water amazed us. Even in fifteen feet, you could see clear down to the white sand bottom.

"South Sea Islands, here we come!" Gale shouted.

Dad stared at a flock of screaming gulls circling the boat. "Sorry, you girls have to take turns pumping. I'll fix that leak for good once we get to Pensacola."

I spent most of my free time that first day riding the bowsprit with Tim perched behind me. When a school of dolphins joined us, we called our parents forward.

"Look at them go!" Mom shouted.

"Why do they keep crisscrossing our bow?" Tim asked. "Aren't they afraid they'll get run over?"

"They do it for fun," Dad said. "Dolphins are playful creatures. Smart, too. They can get up to twenty miles an hour. We're only doing about five."

Dangling our bare feet over the sparkling blue water, Tim and I clapped our hands and shouted encouragement every time one of the silver creatures leaped into the air.

Later, when Mom served lunch in the cockpit, Dad kept talking about Tahiti. "I hope Walter will still be there," he said. "He'll show us around." With his blue-and-white flowered *pareau* slung around his hips, his deep tan, and his straw hat, Dad already looked like a South Sea Islander.

As the *Elizabeth* slowly puttered toward Pensacola, the sun went down, and Dad dropped the anchor. The hot, sultry day gave way to a warm night, and overhead a million stars appeared. Ursa Major, the bear mother, chased her little cub Minor across the sky. After supper, Dad brought out his guitar and started to sing the Tahitian song Walter had taught us. Soon we all joined in. *Un o quatro ha la-bee. Un o quatro ha la-bee.*

Tim announced he was going to take a leak off the transom, but when got there, he jumped backwards.

"Dad! Dad! He shouted. "There's something weird in the water."

When we all rushed to the stern to see, Dad threw a line in the water and swirled it around. Tiny sparks lighted up the water. "It's just phosphorescence," he said. "Plankton."

"Wow, it looks so beautiful!" Gale's voice was hushed as she bent over the stern.

"Like something from outer space," Mom added.

When we first arrived in Pensacola, we stayed at the yacht club. Mom admired the low-slung colonial building and the flowing lawn.

"Pretty ritzy, huh?" She winked.

She also got a big kick out of the way the uniformed dock valet raced down to the boat every weekend when he saw Hempy's Jaguar roaring up the circular driveway.

"He's a-comin' Missy Carole. He's a comin.'"

In a momentary burst of enthusiasm, I'd race down the dock, skirts flying.

Hempy never complained about having to drive all the way from New Orleans to Pensacola, so after a couple of weeks, his visits seemed routine. We'd spend a few minutes talking to Mom and Dad; then we'd find some fabulous new place to eat. Afterwards, we'd drive to the beach. It didn't take long for me to discover that distance had not made my heart grow fonder. Having sex in Hempy's cramped Jaguar made me feel cheap, and ever since we'd left New Orleans, doubts about our engagement kept popping up. Pride kept me from telling my parents how I felt. I knew they would say, *I told you so.*

Because we only had enough money to pay for one month's rent at the yacht club, Dad once again started looking for a cheaper place. In the meantime, I took advantage of all the amenities the yacht club offered. I spent hours in the bathroom, showering and primping. Usually it was empty, but one day another girl was in there, drying her hands under a chrome blower on the wall. She had her back to me, but I could tell she was my age. After setting my clothes and towel down on the sink, I was so busy admiring my deep tan and sun-bleached hair in the mirror, I'd almost forgotten about her. When she came to stand beside me, however, and I saw her face, one big brown scab with two glistening eyes in the middle, I almost screamed.

"Sorry," she said, touching her pinky to her forehead. "I'm Cookie Lutrell. I just had my face sanded. Bad acne. Really bad. "

"Sanded?" I tried to imagine Dad's electrical sander on the girl's forehead.

"It's a new technique. My mother read about it in *Seventeen.*"

"Does it hurt?" I asked.

"Not really. Just itchy." She sighed. "The scabs are supposed to go away in a couple of days, but there's a dance tomorrow night. How am I going to go, if I look like this?"

"Gee, I don't know," I said. "Anyway, I'm Carole Goodlander. My parents own the old schooner at the visitors' dock. We're from Chicago originally, but we're on our way to Tahiti. I think you're really brave to go out at all. I'd probably hide."

"Are you going to the dance?" she asked hopefully.

"No. I'm not a member."

"Well, I am. Go with me. There will be tons of cute Navy guys."

"I'm engaged." I giggled.

"So?" She shrugged. "It's just a dance. It's formal, too. I just bought a new dress. Lilac and white. I'm dying to wear it."

"Oh, it sounds nice, but I don't own a formal."

"That's okay. I have a closet full of them. Come on, you'll enjoy it. Besides if I gross everyone out, I'll need a friend by my side." When Cookie laughed, her whole face transformed. Her big brown eyes twinkled, and I realized in spite of the big scab, she was actually very pretty.

Mom was, of course, thrilled.

"It's the Rose Cotillion!" she panted. "I saw the sign in the yacht club lobby!"

Floating across the lawn in Cookie's lime green and orange chiffon formal, I felt like Cinderella. I'd never worn a strapless dress before, so I felt like a movie star. As I joined the stream of people going into the yacht club, I felt my pulse pounding, so I was glad to find my new friend standing by the front door.

"You look fabulous!" Cookie tucked her arm in mine and pulled me forward.

The yacht club dining room was decorated with a huge mirrored-ball on the ceiling. Banquet tables with red tablecloths and white candles offered platter after platter of food. In the center of each table, glass punchbowls glowed like upside down chandeliers. Swans carved out of ice floated dreamily through orange rinds and strawberries. Pink rose petals were strewn all over the place.

"Look! There's my friend, Bill. Come on, I'll introduce you."

Cookie pulled me onto the dance floor.

"Bill, this is Carole Goodlander. She's just come all the way down the Mississippi on her family's boat."

Dazzled by Cookie's officer friend, the soft formal dress, and the glamorous setting, I spent the whole night wrapped in a sense of enchantment. Bill was a fabulous dancer. Just the sight of him in his gold-buttoned blue military uniform with its crisp, white cap full of gold braid made my knees weak. Prince Charming couldn't have been more attentive or polite. Because the dance didn't end until well after midnight, Bill insisted on walking me back to the boat. As we strolled beneath the rows of leafy trees, he talked about his career, how he was engaged to be married, but the girl was out of town. As we approached the dock, I was wondering if he was going to kiss me, when I saw Hempy's Jaguar parked in the yacht club driveway.

"Oh, I forgot! It's Saturday," I said. "That's my fiancé's car."

"Nice wheels!" Bill whistled and let go of my hand. "I'll say goodnight here, but I hope you'll be around for awhile."

"There's no telling," I shrugged. "I had a really good time tonight."

I was almost to the car when Hempy swung the passenger door open.

"Hop in," he said.

The interior of the car smelled thick with cologne. His shirt looked wrinkled, and sweat stains bled under his arms. As his eyes took in my strapless dress, I felt embarrassed.

"So what's this all about? Who was that guy? I went to the boat. Marie said you'd be home in a few minutes. I've been waiting almost an hour."

"Gee, Hempy, I'm sorry. I forgot it was Saturday. I wasn't even sure you were coming, so when I got invited to the dance...."

"I come every week, don't I?"

After Hempy slammed the Jag into gear, no words passed between us. When we got to the breakwater, he pulled into our usual parking place and turned off the car.

"Hempy, I..." Before I could finish the sentence, he grabbed me by the neck. He pulled me across the seat and kissed me hard; then he shoved his hand under my bra. Usually Hempy was a gentle lover, but that night I felt like I was being mauled by a stranger, so I stopped him.

Pulling away from me, Hempy slumped against the driver-side door. "What's a matter? Still thinking about that officer?"

"No!" I protested.

"Have you screwed him?"

"No!"

"Did you want to?"

Unable to answer that honestly, I started crying.

Hempy's body slid lower in his seat. He looked old, and I didn't like him.

"We're supposed to be engaged, Carole."

"I know, but..."

"No buts about it, baby."

When I saw tears in Hempy's eyes, I wanted to make things right.

"I love you," I sobbed.

"No you don't, Lollipop." Hempy's Adam's apple bobbed up and down. "Your parents were right. It's not your fault. I love you like crazy, but you're just a kid. I should have known better, but hell, baby. I think it would be better if we broke up right now. Feel free to do whatever you want. We're done."

Part of me felt relieved, but another part felt broken. Standing in a cloud of exhaust fumes, watching the Jaguar's red taillights disappear into the night, I felt like falling to the ground.

When I got back to the boat, Mom was pretending to read a book.

"What the heck?" she said. "Did you see Hempy? He was here. I didn't know what to tell him."

My eyes were so swollen I could hardly see. My wet upper lip felt scalded.

"He broke up with me." I wailed. "I hope you're happy now."

"Aw, Carole..." Mom tried to touch my shoulder, but I brushed her hand away. Falling into my bunk, I waited for Gale to say something, but her back was turned away from me.

Muffling my sobs with my pillow, I cried until I couldn't cry anymore. Then I blew my nose and went to sleep.

When Gale and I heard Dad was moving the boat to a dock at the bottom of Palafox Street, the main drag in Pensacola, we were ecstatic. There were so many stores within walking distance and sailors everywhere we looked. I knew my parents had left New Orleans to get me away from Hempy, but to bring me to a place where the whole Navy was waiting? Ha, ha! How stupid was that?

The Warren Fish Company docks were home to a fleet of ancient fishing-smacks with tall wheelhouses on the stern and short masts. Directly across the canal from us, a ramshackle cluster of old wooden buildings housed a dozen stores and bars.

Trader Jon's, one of the most popular watering holes in town, saw hundreds of sailors pass through its door every day. Jon, a legendary beatnik who always wore sandals, wooden beads, and a floppy hat, acted as father confessor, banker, and bartender. Sometimes groups of sailors would wander out to the dock behind the bar. If they saw me on deck in my blue-and-white pareau, whistles and catcalls floated across the water, and though I pretended not to notice, I felt flattered. Cookie visited a couple of times, but she wasn't interested in the sailors who hung around the waterfront. Cookie only went out with officers. "They won't go out with girls who date enlisted man," she warned.

Pensacola was a big town, so Dad hoped to paint a lot of signs. "I can't wait to get a mast," he said. "I hate being a stinkpotter."

Two other people lived aboard their boats at the fish company. One was Captain Fred Mackey, an old salt with a dried apple face. The other was a man everyone called "The Portagee."

Tim followed Captain Fred around like a puppy dog. Deftly sliding fully-rigged, three-masted schooners into tiny bottles, the old man talked a blue streak and his stories were always entertaining.

We never got close to the Portagee because he rarely left his boat, but Mom and I swooned a little every time we saw him. Always dressed in a black turtleneck, with a Greek sailor hat and black pea coat, he wore a gold earring in one ear. When he did go ashore, he usually made a beeline for the big chain-link gate at the entrance to the yard. Mom speculated he might be a wanted man, but Dad said alcoholic or maybe a person with mental problems. Every time our paths crossed, I beamed a big smile at the Portagee, hoping it might cheer him up. It seemed tragic to live like he did, without anybody to talk to or love, but our mysterious neighbor only grunted.

Gale and I had no trouble making friends. Scores of young, homesick, horny sailors swarmed around us like gulls around a trawler unloading fish guts. Sometimes we'd bring the sailors home. They helped Mom carry her groceries, gushed over her home-cooked meals, and confided in her. Dad put all our boyfriends to work. He joked about it, but everyone knew it was true. If they didn't want to help him work on the boat, then forget about it.

A few weeks after we arrived, I walked downtown to find the Walgreen's. What happened with Leroy in Memphis worried me a little, but Pensacola was different because of the Navy base. Everyone got served there, black or white. Afraid I'd get a bad reference, I never mentioned that I worked at a Walgreen's before, so Howie, my boss, was amazed at how fast I caught on to everything. To say I loved my job would be an understatement. Great tips, a nice boss, tons of boyfriends, and, for a change, a team of girls I really liked.

Still reeling from the Hempy episode, I wasn't looking to get serious with anyone, so I went out with dozens of boys, but Vince Cacavarro was my favorite date. Not a boyfriend really, more like a big brother, he was from Massachusetts and homesick for Fall River, his hometown. Once I met Vinnie, I hardly went out with anyone else. Mostly we went to the movies or just walked around town. He did have a car, and that was nice, but I couldn't stay out late because the fish company locked their tall chain-link gate at six o'clock. A friendly watchman named Matt stayed until ten, but after he went home, in order to get to the boat, I had to climb over the fence. Somehow I managed to do this in a very lady-like way, even with crinoline slips and puffy skirts. Putting my toes into the space between links, I'd climb hand over hand to the place where the barbed wire started; then I'd flip my leg over and climb down the other side. Vinnie was used to seeing me do this, but the first time any new date brought me home, he was shocked. One boy from Arkansas peered at me from the other side of the fence. "You looked like a monkey in a dress," he said.

In spite of his finding a lot of signs to paint, Dad's income was still too meager to buy a brand-new mast, so as usual he came up with a brilliant idea. We were all seated in the cockpit, with Mom perched on his lap, when he disclosed his plan. "I've been doing a lot of research," he said. "And guess what I found out? When a wooden light pole gets hit, the electric company has to replace it with a new metal one. They throw the old ones away.

You know how straight and tall those things are? I know I can make a mast out of one, and they sell them dirt cheap."

Mom beamed a big smile at us. "Isn't your dad smart, kids? I mean who else would think to make a mast out of a telephone pole?"

"Well, it will take some work," Dad said. "We'll have to scrape the creosote off and taper it at the top, but I already have a spoke-shave. I'll buy an old sail, and we can steam some mast hoops. In the olden days, all masts were made from trees."

By the time Mickey came to visit that summer, the mast project was in full swing. Gale's boyfriends were put to work getting rid of the creosote. Then we all took turns tapering the pole. It was hard work under a blistering sun, but everyone pitched in. Mickey had barely grabbed his new aqua lung, mask, and flippers from the Greyhound bus that brought him before he was bent over our would-be mast. By the time Dad blew the conch shell to call us for supper, Mickey's body glistened with sweat.

In my cousin's honor, Mom made spaghetti with meat in it. Afterwards we gathered on deck to tell Mickey all the amazing things we'd seen on the Mississippi.

"Wow," he said. "This is nothing like Michigan."

When it came time for bed, he pulled a pair of crisp, baby blue pajamas from his suitcase.

"Where's the shower?" he asked.

"On the dock." Gale grinned. "You have to use the hose. We just stick it down our bathing suits."

"Well, I think I'll just wash up in the head sink then," Mickey said.

Tim shook his head. "It doesn't work."

"You guys are really roughing it, aren't you?" Mickey frowned.

After he pulled his toothbrush from a small zippered bag, he moved toward the galley sink, but Mom stopped him.

"Oh! Don't use that water to brush your teeth. That's tank water. I'll give you some fresh water for that."

Timmy stuck his tongue out. "Tank water tastes like mold."

"Tastes like skunk to me." Gale grimaced.

My cousin looked disappointed when he saw the tiny amount of fresh water Mom poured into his cup, but eventually he disappeared into the head. When he came out wearing his fancy pajamas, it was hard not to laugh.

It didn't take Mickey long to realize living on a boat was no picnic. For one thing, it was hot. Dad had mounted two fans in each hatch, but being from Michigan, Mickey never stopped sweating. "I don't know how you guys can live like this," he panted. "I can't believe you don't have a shower."

Dad hated it when people complained because he thought hardship was a necessary part of adventure. "Sweat is good for you, Mick," he said. "Bathing every day washes all your natural bacteria away. The old timers never used more than a cup of water a day."

By the end of his first week, however, Mickey had assimilated. He had, in fact, stopped wearing shoes and let the peach-fuzz whiskers on his chin and cheeks grow.

"Come on," he said one day. "I want you to peroxide my hair. It will make it look like I've been in the sun longer."

After I'd dumped almost the whole bottle on his head, Mickey's hair went from brown to orange, then pure white.

"Your mother is going to kill you," I said.

After the hair-dying episode, he pulled a pair of new Levis out of his suitcase.

"Got any scissors?" he asked.

When Mom saw Mickey, her eyebrows shot up to her hairline. With his straw-like hair and shredded cutoffs, he looked like someone from a shipwreck.

"It's my new beach-bum look, Aunt Marie, what do you think? Do I look like a Goodlander now?"

One afternoon when I came home from work, I found Mickey sitting cross-legged on the dock with two blocks of wood. He was bare-chested and had a string of wooden beads around his neck. "Remember those Easter Island statues?" he asked. "Let's try to carve some."

When it came time for Dad to teach Mickey to dive, my cousin pulled his aqua lung on deck. He put on his mask and flippers.

"Well, the first thing you have to do, Mickey, is put air in the tank."

"There's no air in there?"

Dad rolled his eyes. "There's no air in there."

"Then, we need to go to a gas station to fill it up."

Dad shook his head. "It's a different kind of air, son."

When Mickey slid into the water, tanks and all, Dad was right beside him. After he showed Mickey how to breathe, the two of them paddled around for a while.

Mickey loved being part of the Goodlander family. His own father, my Uncle Dan, was a short cocky guy, who was always trying to act tough, someone who called Dad "that dumb Indian

son-of-a-bitch". He thought my father was crazy for selling a
going business to move on the boat.

"I love your dad," Mickey told me. "He's like a god to me, a
God of the Sea. What's his name? Neptune? Yeah, Neptune!
Your Dad's always happy. The time I spent upstairs with you guys
were the happiest time of my life. Your dad did things with kids
like a dad should do. Remember how he used to read those Oz
books? He'd sit up there and read the stories. Then, he'd shut off
the lights off, so we could see the stars on the ceiling. Gee, those
were good times. I always wished I had a father like that. "

One day when I went ashore to get groceries, I came home
to find Mickey grinning from ear to ear.

"You look funny," I said. "What's up?"

"I passed the test," he said. "Your dad challenged me. He said
if I was a real Goodlander, I wouldn't be afraid to take my clothes
off. That was the deal. I had to walk naked around the deck twice
then dive in the water. After swimming across the canal, I had to
walk twice around the boat again! "

"You did that?"

"I did! I did it for him," Mickey said. "That's how much
power that man has over me. I'm a real Goodlander now."

The day Mickey left, I had to keep swallowing hard to hold back the tears.

"You've been a good crew member, Mick," Dad said. "Come back when we get to Cuba. We'll have our mast up by then .You can get some real sailing under your belt."

"I will, Uncle Ed. Thanks. I really had fun."

Mom wagged her finger at him. "You be sure and tell your mother, Mickey, that I never approved of you dying your hair."

One afternoon when Dad was painting a board to mend the cockpit, I reached my hand out to help steady it. Noticing the circle of white skin on my ring finger, he frowned. "So what ever happened to Hempy's ring? I hope you gave it back to him?"

"I didn't have time. He left in such a hurry. I was going to mail it, but that didn't seem right. I was thinking of asking Cookie to go to New Orleans with me, so I could return it in person. We could take a bus. Do you think it would be okay if we stayed at Walter's place?"

"Hopefully, Walter is almost to Tahiti by now," Dad said. "But I'm sure Albert is still there. I suggest you do this right away, Carole. You wouldn't want Hempy to think you're going to keep it."

When I asked Cookie, she jumped at the chance. "I'd love to go! I've been thinking about buying a guitar. I bet with all the musicians in New Orleans the pawn shops are full of them."

The day Cookie and I climbed aboard the Greyhound bus, I felt excited. As the scenery slid by, I kept pulling the blue-velvet box from my purse, snapping it open to stare at the diamond.

"You better put that thing away," Cookie warned. "Someone might want to steal it."

It was late afternoon when we got to the French Quarter, and it felt good to once again be walking beneath its wrought-iron balconies. When we got to Bourbon Street, Cookie kept stopping to gawk at the strip club posters. "Do you think their breasts are really that big?" She giggled. "I've always wanted to see a strip-show." She'd moved to the door for a peek, when two good-looking older men in shiny blue suits approached.

"You girls going inside?"

"We can't," Cookie said. "We're under-age."

"Hey, this is New Orleeeeans!" The tall guy with the blonde crew cut put his arm around Cookie's waist. "They won't care. C'mon. You'll see. No problem."

The inside of the club was dark. The music was loud. Only the stage was lighted. In the middle of it, a dancer with long blonde hair, wearing a cat mask squatted on a leopard skin platform. Clutching both her breasts in her hands, she rotated gold tassels on the end of them in slow circles.

"Four bourbons and water," our escort told the waitress.

Cookie and I grinned at each other. Man, were we lucky or what? Not only were these guys cute, but they were also buying.

The dark-haired guy tossed a pack of Luckies on the table. "I'm Frank," he said. "That's Steve."

Cookie and I drank our bourbons quickly, and we didn't protest when Frank ordered more. Fascinated by the swirling lights and the almost naked stripper, I wasn't counting. At one point, I saw Steve pull his chair next to Cookie's. He was kissing her neck, and she was laughing.

Every time Cat Woman, one of New Orleans' most famous strippers, paraded across the stage, the crowd hooted and howled. When she started humping the long, black tail she pulled between her legs, the crowd went wild. Putting one hand over her eyes, Cat Woman peered into the audience and purred. "Meow.... meow.... Are there any tomcats out there?"

When Steve leaped up on our table, he almost knocked it over. Squatting on all fours, he titled his face toward the ceiling, and started to howl like a cat in pain. When the red spotlight that had been dizzily washing over the room hit him, he stood straight up and howled even louder.

After Steve sat down again, everyone started buying him drinks. At one point, when Cookie reached for hers, she backhanded mine, and my empty glass fell to the floor. When I reached down to get it, the room started spinning so fast I could barely focus. Realizing things were getting out of hand, I tried to stand, but my legs felt like seaweed. Clutching the table for support, I inched my way over to Cookie.

"Hey, you girls want to come back to our hotel?" Steve asked.

"I need to go to the ladies room," I said.

"I'll go with you." Cookie smiled.

Once we were alone, I suggested we leave.

"I'm way too drunk."

"Me, too!" Cookie giggled.

"Well, we'd better get out of here then. Let's not say goodbye."

"Right!" Cookie was leaning against the wall for support. "No goodbyes."

Pulling my friend by the hand, I skirted the edges of the bar. Just before I opened the door to a world full of blinding sunlight,

I glanced back at our table, but Frank and Steve were busy talking.

The warm air outside the bar smelled like coffee and hops. We were headed for Toulouse, but Cookie saw some kids tap-dancing at the corner of Bourbon and Dumaine, so she insisted we stop. Sitting on the curb, the two of us tried pulling ourselves together. Cookie slipped a brush from her purse, and I smoothed my skirt. When the kids were done dancing, the crowd clapped, and everyone started to throw money into a hat on the sidewalk. I wanted to give something too, but that's when I realized my purse was gone.

"Oh, my God!" I grabbed Cookie's arm. "I left my purse! We have to go back! Quick!"

Racing back to the bar, I felt my stomach spinning. It only took a few minutes to get there, but our table was empty.

The waitress who had brought our drinks saw us standing there. "If you're looking for those two guys you were with, they're gone," she said.

"Gone? But I left my purse hanging on my chair. Did they turn it in?"

"They didn't say anything about a purse."

"Take it off! Take it all off!" The crowd behind us screamed.

Cookie and I staggered back outside where I puked with one hand against a wall. "How am I ever going to explain this to Hempy," I sobbed. "Or my father?"

Cookie's fingertips pulled my hair back from my face. Opening her purse, she handed me a Kleenex. "I'm so sorry, Carole. We never should have gone in there. But it'll be okay. You don't *have to* return the ring. A lot of girls keep them. "

"They got all my money and my bus ticket home too."

"Don't worry. I have enough to pay for both of us," Cookie said, "but shouldn't we call the police?"

"We don't even know their full names, and we're underage. I'm sure they'd never find them anyway, so what's the point?"

Because I didn't want to go to Albert's until we'd sobered up, I took Cookie over to Café Du Monde.

"What were we thinking?" Cookie moaned over her white mug.

"We weren't," I said.

After a few cups of strong coffee, things seemed almost normal, so we headed once again to Bourbon Street. This time though we didn't stop anywhere or speak to anyone. A flood of relief hit me as we turned into the cool shadowy corridor running alongside 912.

That night Albert lectured us about trusting men we didn't know, but he was glad to see me. Exhausted from all the stress, all I wanted to do was lie down.

Pointing to his big iron bed, Albert said, "You girls can sleep with me. I'm harmless."

When I woke the next morning, sun was shining through the window. Albert had one arm around my waist and next to him, Cookie was snoring. I was just about to get up when the door opened and a tiny man wearing a beret popped in. Albert lifted his head.

"Whoa!" The man chuckled. "I didn't know you had company." He took a few steps into the room and threw his hands in the air. "Mon Dieu! You are not Albert. I would call you Lucky Pierre!"

On the bus-ride home, Cookie played her new guitar. She tried to get me to sing with her, but my spirits were too low. Leaning my head against the window, watching the blurred landscape, I wished I never had to go home.

"Do you really expect me to believe a cock-and-bull story like that?" Dad's fists rested on his hips. "You pawned the damn thing didn't you?"

"I did not! It was stolen! Ask Cookie!"

"Well, of course, your friend would back you up, but I think you're lying. I think you pawned the ring and spent the money. I suppose this is between you and Hempy, but, really, you ought to be ashamed of yourself, Carole. It was a rotten thing to do to someone who has always been so nice to you."

A few nights later, when I went ashore to smoke a cigarette, I ran into the night watchman. He knew I smoked. Sometimes when it rained, he let me smoke in his office.

"What's up kiddo?"

When I told him about the New Orleans disaster, Matt rubbed his temples with his fists.

"Ain't nothing worse than guilt," he said.

Matt told me he'd had been married once to a woman named Jenny who died in a car accident. A blow-out caused her to lose control. After the car hit a guard rail, it flipped over and caught fire. Jenny was four months pregnant at the time, and Matt blamed himself.

"Isn't a man supposed to take care of things like that?"

Pulling his hand through his hair, Matt stomped on his cigarette butt, grinding it into the ground. We become close friends after that.

On my seventeenth birthday he gave me a Siamese kitten. I couldn't believe he remembered me saying I adored Siamese cats, but there it was in a little box on his desk.

When I showed the kitten to Mom, she stroked its soft ears. "These pure breeds cost a lot," she said.

Ironically, a week after I got my kitten, a stray, white cat with torn ears and a large scar across its face showed up, and Gale decided we should adopt it. In spite of it being a girl cat, Gale named her "The Dude". More agile than Penrod, Gale's feisty cat terrorized him. Mom said The Dude was tough because she was a wharf cat. Pedigree sometimes made people stupid. The worst part was Penrod's big testicles. The Dude running up behind him, thumped on those little sacs like a prizefighter fighter hitting a punching bag. Poor Penrod!

One night when I went to look for my sweetie, I couldn't find him anywhere. I was on shore calling his name when a fisherman named Michigan Jack heard me.

"Looking for that fancy brown cat?"

"Yeah, have you seen him?"

"The gars got him," Michigan Jack said. "Saw him floating in the canal yesterday. He was all tore up. Must of fell in the water. I seen that white cat chasing him around."

I hated telling Matt what happened, but he said it wasn't my fault.

"It's hard losing things you love," he said, "but what's the choice? Not ever loving anything?"

At that point, I felt so sad about what happened with Hempy, the ring and the cat, the thought of not loving anything ever again seemed like a good idea.

In order to not think about all my problems, I threw myself into my job. Two of the girls I worked with at Walgreen's were a lot of fun. Alicia Marie and Linda Jane were sisters, but they looked nothing alike. One was blonde and short, the other was tall and dark. Both of them were loud and boy crazy, but I found them admirable because they knew what they wanted and they went for it. They even had their own apartment a few blocks from work. Every night a bunch of sailors would wait outside to see who would walk them home. I felt envious of their ability to support themselves, in spite of the fact that according to them the family they came from was "just a bunch of nuts and drunks".

One day in June, Linda Jane said she and her sister were looking for a roommate. Did I want to move in? I never would have considered moving off the boat, but Dad had started pushing me to pay room and board. He said the extra money would help pay for the sail we needed to make our Gulf passage, but I took it as a punishment for losing Hempy's ring.

"Pay rent to live aboard the *Elizabeth*? I'll have to think about that," I said. "A couple of girls at work have been asking me to move in with them. It would be cheaper, and I'd have my own room."

I knew Dad felt wounded. Moving off the boat was right up there with treason and divorce. I expected him to express disgust or disappointment, but all he did was shrug. "Suit yourself, Carole," he said. "Go live among the Dreamchrushers for awhile. You'll see."

I planned my departure for a time when I knew Dad was working. I wanted to feel excited, but when it came time to pack up my stuff and say goodbye, I almost changed my mind.

"Bye, Carole." Tim hung his arms around my neck

Gale had already started gathering her Indian books for the big move. "Mom said I can have your shelf." Her voice sounded happy, but her eyes told a different story.

"You guys can visit me anytime," I said. "My room is big. Maybe you can spend the night."

"I really wish you wouldn't do this, Carole." Mom looked like she was going to cry. "I'm sure your father thinks you'll come right back. I know he's upset about this."

The room the sisters gave me had polished wood floors and an arched window with a big beautiful banyan tree heavy with Spanish moss right outside. To cheer myself up, I bought a yellow bedspread, a blue rug, and a small portable radio. Waking up in the morning with sunlight flooding across my bed, I couldn't help but imagine how envious Gale would be---Mom too, probably. Life ashore meant running water, high ceilings, and real furniture. Life on the *Elizabeth* meant a head that never worked, one little bookshelf, and a bunk so short I'd learned to sleep all curled up.

One hot summer night, my friend Vinnie and I decided to drive to the beach.

"I need to go back to the base to get my bathing suit," he said. "I also want to say goodbye to a friend who is leaving."

As we pulled up to the curb beside Vinnie's barracks, he smiled.

"Oh, good, he's still here."

"Who?" I asked.

"Joe Borges. That's the guy. He's being sent to the chain gang tonight."

"The chain gang?" I gasped. "They still have those? What did he do murder somebody?"

"No!" Vinnie laughed. "Joe's a good guy. He got drunk one night with a bunch of friends who wanted to steal hubcaps. Joe didn't even have a car. He was so drunk he passed out. When he woke up, he saw his friends were in a fight with some white-hairs. His buddy Fish was on the ground, getting kicked in the head, so Joe jumped out. He cold-cocked a bunch of them before they took him down. Talk about bad luck. It turned out to be a Pinellas Park sheriff's convention."

A feeling of sadness came over me when I thought about how unfair things were sometimes. Like when a person gets accused of hocking a ring or has to pay rent to live with her own family.

"But why did he get arrested? He wasn't stealing the hubcaps."

"Assault and battery," Vinnie said. "It didn't matter. Theft from a motor vehicle, too. His friends were locals. Their families hired lawyers. Joe was the only one that didn't get off. He ended up taking the rap for all of them."

"He must be really pissed," I said. "And scared."

Vinnie shook his head. "Nah, not Joe. He doesn't let anything get him down. He's a Steve McQueen kind of guy."

Watching Vinnie walk across the lawn to the barracks, I tried to imagine life on a chain gang. Shackles and guns, snarling dogs, hard-core criminals ready to explode at any time? Swallowing hard, I saw Vinnie shake his friend's hand, then throw his arms around him.

A few weeks later, I was waiting for Vinnie to walk me home from work. When he didn't show up, I started to worry. It was almost closing time, so I started to move the THIS SECTION IS CLOSED sign across the entrance to the dining room, but a customer stopped me.

"Are you Carole?"

A white T-shirt barely contained the boy's muscular chest. His Sylvester the Cat tattoo looked new. "Do I know you?"

"I'm Joe Borges, a friend of Vinnie's. He's been put on restriction for speeding, so he won't be able to leave the base. He asked me to stop by here, so you'd know. Ten days."

"It's quitting time," I said. "I only live a few blocks away. You can walk me home and tell me all about it."

As the afternoon sun slid into Pensacola Bay and the heat of the day retreated, we wove our way through streams of people walking down Palafox Street. Joe Borges had an aura about him, a way of parting the crowds of people rushing toward us. There was no moment of falling in love. It was more like the sky opened its blue eye to expose a heaven I'd never imagined. Joe was a magnet, and I was a pile of iron shavings. We had already rounded the corner to my apartment, when I finally found enough courage to ask him about the chain gang.

"Was it awful?"

Joe rubbed his fingertips across his eyebrows. "Well, they worked us like dogs all day," he said, "but at night we could pretty much do whatever we wanted. A couple of the men played guitar. Some had harmonicas. That was cool. The grub was great. In spite of all the hard work, I gained ten pounds."

We'd almost reached the house when a car came wheeling close to the curb beside me. Joe steered me away from the street.

"Girls are supposed to walk on the inside," he said

"They are?" I asked. "Why?"

"For protection," he said, like I was something that needed to be defended.

Climbing the stairs to the apartment, I could sense Joe right behind me. My hands shook when I pulled the keys from my purse. We entered the kitchen through the back door, and I was relieved my roommates weren't home.

"I used to be a tree-cutter." Joe nodded toward the banyan tree outside the window. "It was one of my first jobs. It was dangerous, so you had to stay focused." He shook his head and laughed. "My mind was always someplace else. The guys on the crew nicknamed me *Trance.* It was embarrassing."

"I share this apartment," I said. "Two girls from work. They're nice, but they party too much. I like quiet. I used to live on a boat. Weekends here are crazy. It's like the whole Navy shows up. I usually stay in my room."

"You lived on a boat?"

"It's docked at the Warren Fish Docks across from Trader Jon's. I miss my family, but my father wanted me to pay room and board. All I had was a bunk and one shelf. It was cheaper to move in here."

"You lived on it full time? Doesn't your family have a house?"

"No. My Dad wants to sail to Tahiti. He's sick of the rat race. He's a little weird, but I love him. Hey, you want a cup of coffee?"

"Sure." Joe smiled. "I'm a fiend."

"Me, too!" I laughed.

After I set our cups on the table, I slid into the chair next to Joe. When our knees touched, a school of silver dolphins leaped around my heart.

After Joe told me all about Vinnie's problem, he looked at the clock on the wall. I didn't want him to leave, so I said I wanted to write Vinnie a note. "It'll just take a minute."

"Sure," he said.

For a long time, we just sat there gawking at one another.

"Oh, yeah," I said. "The note paper is in my room. Want to have a tour of the house?"

As we moved toward the front living room, I was hoping my roommates had picked-up before they left, but the windowsills still had empty beer bottles on them. Clothes and magazines were thrown in a pile on the couch, and every ashtray was full.

"Sorry about the mess." I grabbed a few bottles and threw them in a wastebasket next to the couch. "On a boat there's a place for everything and everything is always in its place. These girls never put anything away."

When I opened the door to my closet to get my note paper, the colorful drawings taped to the back of it fluttered. "I keep my stationary in here," I said.

"Did you draw those pictures?"

"They were here when I moved in. Kids I guess. Aren't they cute? I can draw. I had some great teachers in New Orleans. I hope to be an artist someday."

Joe moved closer. "I like kids," he said.

When I tuned to look at him, Joe's cheek almost brushed mine. Without saying a word, he put his arm around my waist and kissed me. It was smooth and sweet, like a white-sand beach with warm water lapping at the edges.

Joe took a step backwards. "Oh, sorry!" He raised his hands palm-out against his chest and shook his head. "You're Vinnie's girl. I shouldn't have done that. He's my friend."

"No, I'm not!"

"Well, I got the impression..."

"He's not my boyfriend."

"Well, still..." Joe rubbed his hands on his jeans. He pulled a pack of Chesterfield's from his rolled-up sleeve, lighted a cigarette and sat on the bed. "You'd better write your note."

Scribbling away on a sheet of lined, yellow paper, I told Vinnie I was sorry that he was put on restriction. I also told him that I liked Joe Borges a lot and hoped he liked me too.

When I opened the back door, I wanted Joe to kiss me again, but he didn't.

"If it is okay with Vinnie, Carole, I'll come by your work tomorrow."

At first I couldn't believe Joe Borges was really interested in me. He was after all one of the most poplar guys in his barracks. Everyone respected him. With Hempy, I was the adored one, the one being pursued, but now the tables were turned. When he said my name, it was like no one had ever said it before, each syllable a caress and a claim. Joe owned me, and I owned him. With his strong cheekbones, curly black hair, and athletic body, he reminded me of the Greek statues I'd seen in the museums in Chicago.

Joe didn't think he was handsome though. Pointing to a barely visible, white line cutting through his left eyebrow, he told me he'd been in a car accident before he joined the Navy. "The doctor who sewed me up back in Taunton did a lousy job. Last year the Navy tried to fix it. At least the big blobs are gone, but I still look like a monster."

"You can't even see it," I said. "You have a beautiful face."

Joe put his arm around me. "You're the one who is beautiful. I've had other girlfriends, Carole, but none of them were as pretty as you."

Joe and I spent all our free time together. Sometimes we hung out with Vinnie or one of Joe's other friends, but mostly we liked being alone in my apartment. Because of my roommates constant partying that didn't happen often. Even though my room was at the end of a long hall, their loud music made it almost impossible to talk. Some nights we couldn't even get to the bathroom without having to push our way through a line of sailors. One night when things got especially loud, Joe got mad. "Come on, "he said. "Let's get the hell out of here."

In the back yard, one of the banyan tree's branches swooped low to the ground. Joe hoisted himself up and pulled me alongside him. The draped strands of Spanish moss hanging in front us, hid us from view.

`"Now isn't this better?" Joe leaned back against the old tree. "We have our own private room."

From that night on, whenever my roommates threw a party, Joe and I would spend most of the night in our tree. Like two love birds, we fluttered around our feelings, slowly peeking away any doubts we had about our future together. We swapped bits and pieces of our lives and confessed our dreams.

One day Joe said it out loud. "I love you, Carole."

"I love you too, Joe."

Naturally, I was dying to tell Mom I had met the man of my dreams, but pride kept me from returning to the *Elizabeth*. I hadn't seen my family for more than two months, but now I felt an urge to visit. One morning when Joe was on duty and couldn't leave the base, I decided to go home. As I walked toward the waterfront, I kept wondering how everyone would react. Did they miss me? Would Dad still be mad? When I got to the fish company gate, I glanced toward the dock, but it was empty. Had they left without saying anything?

I was standing there stunned, when Rick the Stick came along.

"Where's my boat, Rick? Where's my family?"

"Don't worry, they ain't left without ya." Rick grinned a snaggle-toothed smile. "They went to get gas. I guess they are leaving pretty soon though. Ain't you goin' with 'em?"

I hung around the docks until it was time for me to go to work, but the boat never came back. Filled with remorse, I wanted to tell Dad I wanted to come back home, that I couldn't bear it if they left without me, but what about Joe? How could I ever leave him?

"We're going away for a few days," Linda Jane said. "We're leaving Saturday. Howie said you might take a few of our shifts."

"Sure! No problem," I said. "Joe and I will have the apartment all to ourselves."

On Saturday the sun was shining, but a cool breeze coming off the Gulf brought some relief from the hot spell we'd been having. Getting up early, I went downtown to buy a copy of *The Betty Crocker Cooking for Two Cookbook* I'd been eyeing in the bookstore window. Excited to know we'd have the house to ourselves for two whole days, I planned to serve Joe a special dinner. I also bought a bouquet of bright yellow flowers..

A few hours later, when he saw the pretty table I'd set, Joe let out a low whistle.

"Wow! Nice!" What smells so delicious? "

I blushed when he kissed my neck.

"I'm making meat loaf," I said. "I hope it turns out okay."

Usually Joe wore civilian clothes when he was off the base, but that day he was in full Navy blues.

"I didn't have time to change," he said. "It's a good thing I left an extra pair of Levis here."

"Well, hurry up," I told him. "All I have to do is mash the potatoes."

Waltzing over to the table with my perfect looking meat loaf, I felt proud.

"Come on. Dinner is ready, Joe."

"I'll be right there." He answered from the bedroom.

I'd just put the mashed potatoes on the table, when a loud thud shook the whole house. The back door flew open, and three men barged into the house.

"Police! Stay right there! Don't move! Put your hands up!"

My body was shaking so badly, I could hardly lift my arms. One of the detectives pulled a gun from a shoulder holster. He was sweeping it around the room, when Joe appeared.

"Stop! Hold it right there."

Naked to the waist and barefoot, Joe looked ready to fight. "Who the hell are you?" he said.

One of the taller cops flashed his badge at me. "You're under arrest," he said, "for running a disorderly house." Then, he turned to Joe. "Where are your clothes, son?"

Joe rubbed a hand across his bare chest. He looked down at his bare feet. "My shirt is in the bedroom," he said. "I was just changing into civvies."

"Well, we're charging you with indecent exposure. Both of you have the right to remain silent. Anything you say can and will be used against you in a court of law. You have a right to an attorney. If you cannot afford an attorney, one will be appointed for you."

They let me turn the stove off and get my purse before they shuffled us down the back stairs. In broad daylight, I kept my head down. Shame burned through my body. I realized there were plenty of times when the noise in the house might have caused someone to call the cops, but not that day. And running a disorderly house? What did that mean?

They put Joe and I in separate squad cars. I kept protesting my innocence, but the detectives said they had a witness, an old man in a wheelchair, who lived on the second floor of the house across the street. Apparently he had been watching our apartment. He said sailors were coming and going all day and night. The music was so loud he couldn't sleep. He'd also witnessed underage drinking. In his mind, we were prostitutes doing a bang-up business.

"It's not what you think! Please...listen..." I sobbed. "My roommates can be rowdy, but they're not prostitutes. My boyfriend and I stay in my room. There's a tree behind the house and...."

After being fingerprinted and booked, I was put in a cell with three other women. They looked tough. One was huddled in the corner, the other two sat on a bunk. *Real prostitutes.* A sink with a drinking fountain hung on one wall. Feeling thirsty, I started walking toward it, but one of the women grabbed me by the arm. I thought my heart was going to stop. "Don't drink from there!" she said. "You look like a nice girl. You could get trench mouth." I didn't know what trench mouth was, but it sounded ugly. Feeling scared, I sank to the floor and put my head on my knees.

A little while later, an officer came to tell me I had the right to make one phone call. He said bail had been set at five hundred dollars. I had no clue what bail was, so he explained that I'd only have to pay fifty dollars. But, I only had a ten on me. Payday was still two days away, so how was I supposed to get enough money to get out? Not wanting to call my father, I decided to call Howie. My boss liked me. He needed me. Maybe he'd pay my bail?

"Tough luck, babe," Howie said. "I'll send someone right over, but what happened?"

"I'll explain later. Just don't say anything to anyone. Please, Howie. My parents will die if they ever find out about this."

When I got to the front desk to collect my things, I asked the clerk about Joe.

"The Navy came and got him a while ago."

As I walked back to town, I kept thinking about the old man in the wheelchair. Anger brought tears to my eyes. I wanted to blame everything on my wild roommates, but how could I do that? I'd stayed in the apartment because I want to be with Joe, but never in my wildest dreams did I imagine something like this could happen!

When I stopped by Walgreen's to thank Howie, I learned there was a warrant out for Linda Jane and Alicia Marie, but they hadn't come back to town yet. Howie said I'd probably see them in court, but I never saw those girls again.

When I got back to the apartment, I started to clean the kitchen, but I was crying so hard my eyes got all blurry. My meatloaf still sat in the middle of the table, but a dozen flies were buzzing around it. The pretty flowers, I'd arranged so carefully, drooped over the lip of their vase, and I felt scared and alone. Hanging a blanket across the front window, I saw the old man's face in the window across the street. How could he? How dare he? I knew I was innocent, but would that mean anything in a court of law?

I expected to see my roommates in the court room, but only Joe was there. An official looking naval officer wearing a flat hat with gold braid sat with him at a long wooden table in front of the judge's bench. When I came in, Joe looked up. He smiled, but I could tell he was worried. Every time he and the Navy lawyer put their heads together, Joe picked at his scar.

When the judge found me guilty, I wept. The fine was fifty dollars, so I was glad I'd accepted the money Howie had offered the night before. I kept telling him I wouldn't need it because I was innocent, but he insisted.

"Just in case," he said, tucking the bills into my apron.

Joe was guilty, too, but he only had a thirty dollar fine. On our way out of the court room, he managed to tell me they were going to put him in the brig. They were also going to court martial him. That would take a while, but eventually a dishonorable discharge was inevitable.

"Too many bad things have happened," he said. "The Navy considers you AWOL when you're in jail. All that time I spent on the chain-gang and now this. I'll come see you as soon as I can."

"I'm sorry, Joe." I mumbled. "I'm so sorry. This is all my fault."

That night the hollow emptiness of the apartment kept me from sleeping. I kept hearing noises. I knew the downstairs door was locked, but what if some of my roommates' friends came by? When I thought about Joe, I felt terrible. Would the Navy really give him a dishonorable discharge, and if they did? What would that mean? What would happen to us? I'd already decided to move back on the boat, but what would I tell my parents?

The next day, I was sitting on the bedroom floor packing up my stuff. Shoving what I wanted into a pillowcase, I felt overwhelmed. If my roommates weren't coming back, where was I supposed to leave my keys and what about their stuff? The thoughts in my head buzzed so loud, I didn't even hear the back door open. I didn't realize my parents were there, until they stood right in front of me.

"Oh, you surprised me!" I tried to smile. "What are you doing here?"

"We went to your work last night." Mom's eyes scanned the room. "We're leaving Pensacola the first of the month. We wanted to tell you, but you weren't there."

Dad plunked himself down on my bed. "Your boss told us what happened," he said. "Don't you be mad at him either. He did the right thing. Parents have a right to know what's happening with their kids. Get your things together. You're coming home with us right now."

Mom's eyes looked puffy and red. Her arms hung limp at her sides, and she looked old.

"It wasn't my fault. Didn't Howie tell you? It was all a big mistake."

Walking back to the boat, I knew I was too old to skip, but that's what I felt like doing. Knowing I was going back to the *Elizabeth* where everything was orderly and contained made me dizzy with relief. Dad had been right about shore-life. Things were too complicated there, too uptight and unreasonable. Surely there were no stupid laws about indecent exposure or running a disorderly house in Tahiti. Heck, they went around half-naked all the time, and sailors came and went as they pleased.

That night sitting on deck, enjoying the familiar gurgle of water slapping quietly against the boat's hull, I was surprised when Dad came to sit beside me. He put his arm around me and turned my chin with his hand. Looking directly into my eyes, he smiled. "I want you to remember this, Carole. No matter how stormy the night, I'll always love you. I'll always be your father."

Except for the fact that Gale gave a little groan when I took back my shelf, everyone seemed glad I was home. Tim followed me around like a puppy dog, and Mom kept saying I seemed more grown-up. The next day when Dad asked me to help make some mast hoops for the almost-finished mast, I jumped at the chance.

Arranging a pile of scrap wood under a discarded hot water heater he'd found in the fish company's dumpster, Dad had me feed the fire under it. "Once it gets steaming hot, we'll put the wood for the hoops inside. The steam will make it bend like butter. They have to be perfectly round, in order to slide easily up and down the mast, so I built a jig. In the olden days, sailors didn't have sail track. Hoops work just fine."

Two weeks passed with no word from Joe. At work I couldn't keep my eyes off the front door. Howie said if he was discharged, they'd give him a ticket home, but I couldn't imagine him leaving town without saying goodbye.

The day I looked up from the lunch counter to see Joe striding towards me, it took everything I had not to run across the floor, to throw myself in his arms. Untying my apron, I told Howie I was going to take a break. Grabbing Joe's hand, I pulled him into a booth.

"I missed you like crazy! What happened? Are they going to discharge you?"

"Probably," he said. "The brig was worse than the chain-gang. Those MPs really try to bust a guy's balls. The Navy is going to give me a dishonorable discharge. Shit! That stinks. Everyone says I ought to fight it, but I'm not going to."

"Well, what will you do then?"

"Go home, I guess," he said. "I hate facing my family."

"Oh, no, you can't go home! I've been thinking about this a lot. I had to move back on the boat. We're leaving soon, but I'll ask my dad if you can come with us. Once he knows how I feel about you, he'll say yes. I know he will."

Joe frowned. "Oh, sure, he'll love that idea. Some reject from the Navy? Why would he want me there?"

"Because I love you! We love each other, right? Besides he can use an extra hand."

"But I've never even been on a boat."

"You haven't? But you're in the Navy?"

"I'm in naval air, Carole." Joe shrugged. "I work on airplanes."

"Well, that's okay. You're strong. You can be our crew."

Joe hung his head. "It's a nice thought, Carole. I don't want to leave you, either. I want us to be together, but your dad will never go for it."

When I first approached my father, he was priming the mast, and he was dead set against my plan.

"We don't even know this guy," he said. "If the Navy discharged him there must have been a good reason. You haven't known him all that long. He might be a troublemaker. "

"I told you it wasn't his fault. Look what happened to me. The cops down here are crazy. It's like a police state or something."

Dad shook his head. "Dreamcrushers," he said. "I heard they arrested an old lady from New jersey for jaywalking last week. Gave them some lip, I guess. Wrestled her to the ground, too. It was all over the papers."

"Joe is a good kid." I said. "He'd be a big help. Lots of boats take a crew with them. Come on, Dad. This isn't like with Hempy. I love Joe. I really love him, and he's too ashamed to go home."

Dad finished the prime coat and stood back. "Well, bring him around. I'll talk to him. It does sound like he got a raw deal. An extra hand wouldn't hurt."

When I told Joe that Dad wanted to meet him, he seemed hopeful.

"Really?"

The day I brought Joe home, Dad was putting a finish coat on the mast. As we passed through the fish company gate, I grabbed Joe's hand. It felt sweaty. He kept rubbing his fingers across his forehead.

When he saw us coming, Dad laid the paintbrush across his can and stood up straight. He was six foot three and almost three hundred pounds. "What's this I hear about you sleeping with my daughter?" he said.

I flinched.

"Uh, well, I...uh..."

"Forget it," Dad said. "It sounds like the Dreamchrushers have been trying to do a number on you. Carole wants you to move aboard. What do you think about that?"

"I don't want her to leave here without me." Joe looked around the fish company yard. Then, he nodded toward the mast. "Is that the mast you made yourself? It sure doesn't look like a telephone pole."

Dad's eyes brightened. Looking Joe up and down, he grabbed an extra brush and handed it to him. "Do you know how to paint?"

"I do," Joe said. "My grandfather taught me. He bought an old house, and we fixed it up. I helped him do the plumbing and heating, the electric, too. We did everything ourselves. I like working with my hands."

When Joe started painting, Dad noticed his smooth stroke. When he loaded his brush and slapped it confidently against the rim of the can, my father smiled. "Go tell your Mom and the kids that Joe is here. She made some sandwiches for lunch."

After Joe moved aboard everything in our life seemed more exciting. His enthusiasm to learn how to be a good sailor and his excitement about joining our life away from the rat race, away from anything he had ever known, gave second wind to Dad's dream.

"Your father is amazing," Joe said. "I've never met anyone like him. He knows everything, and he's happy all the time. He follows his dreams and doesn't care what anyone else thinks."

"I had a lot of misgivings about bringing Joe aboard," Dad said, "but I like him a lot. He's not afraid of work, and he seems very serious about you."

Mom said Joe looked just like Ricky Nelson. "He combs his hair the same way, but Joe's got bigger muscles."

Tim loved having Joe around. Mom and us girls treated Tim like a baby, but Joe roughhoused with him, he encouraged a masculine recklessness that even Dad didn't have. He was always saying: *Go for it, Tim! Go for it!* Like when Tim kept riding his training wheels bicycle off the end of the dock. Pedaling faster and faster, he'd fly into the air, then come splashing down with a thud. Even after he hit the water, Tim never let go of the handlebars. Sometimes I worried, but a few minutes later, my little brother's head would emerge in a burst of spray.

"Would you mind diving down to get it, Joe?"

"Sure, kid." Joe always pretended like Tim's Evel Knievel trick was an accident.

Joe seldom spoke about his family back in Massachusetts, but I knew he had two little brothers named Ronnie and Jeep. "I wonder if they miss me," Joe said. "I have a sister Diane, too. She's studying to be a nurse. We were close."

Tim and I spent all our spare time fishing. At first, we felt squeamish about baiting our hooks, so Joe took over that part. One day sitting at the end of the dock, Tim leaned against Joe. "I love you, Joey," he said. "I'm so glad you came with us."

"I love you too, Timmy. Now, get your fish-gut fingers out of my hair."

Gale, of course, was secretly in love with Joe. "He rolls me a couple of cigarettes every day," she grinned. "Then he hides them under his hat, so I can find them. It's a kind of pact we have. You're not supposed to know."

When the mast was finally done, Dad recruited a couple of fishermen to help set it in place. Taking a gold coin from his pocket, he turned it over and over.

"Before I slide the mast in, I want you to set this under it. It's an old tradition that goes all the way back to the Greeks. Sailors back then always put a gold coin under the mast to be sure they had enough money to pay Charon, this guy with a ferry. In case somebody on board died, he'd have to row them across the River Styx to the Land of the Dead."

Standing on shore, Mom, Gale and Tim cheered when the mast thudded into place.

"Okay!" Dad hitched up his *pareu* and slapped his straw hat against his thigh. "We're ready to go now, Marie!"

A few days before we left Pensacola, I quit my job, so I could help with last minute preparations. Howie hated to see me leave, but he was nice about it. "Hey, you're the best girl I have," he said. "If you ever need a reference let me know."

While Dad and Joe were busy building some new shelves for the tool room, Gale and I cleaned out the bilge, so Mom could store her can goods in there. Soon we'd be entering the wide waters of the Gulf, and things could get pretty rough out there.

"Make sure everything is lashed down good," Dad said. "A lot of injuries can happen from stuff flying around. A loose can of soup can break somebody's nose. We sure don't need any broken bones at sea."

At night the family gathered around the dinette table laughing and joking. We studied the colorful Gulf of Mexico charts. We learned how to read the depth of the water and where navigation lights were placed. Mom showed us pictures of the birds and fish we could expect to see. Sometimes, living aboard the *Elizabeth* was like being on a scientific expedition. Dad said, "See Marie. The kids are learning more living aboard, than they'd ever learn in school."

Knowing once we went to sea, we'd never get a chance to be alone, Joe and I couldn't wait for night to come. After our work was done, we'd walk over to Cry Beach, a desolate little spot tucked into a crook of weedy shoreline. Winos and homeless people frequented the debris strewn beach, so at first I was scared to make love there, but Joe's pleading always got the best of me. Besides, the only other place we ever had sex was under an old railroad car rusting on a set of weedy tracks behind the fish house. Cry Beach was not ideal, but the tender sex we had there made it very appealing.

When Joe first moved aboard, Dad told him he'd have to sleep on deck. "You can rig up a piece of canvas to make a tent," he said. "We have an air mattress. If it rains you can move into the dinette, but just for the night. You two aren't married, so there's no way you're sleeping together. As long as you're living here, Joe, I expect you to show respect. No sex. And I mean that too. I'm keeping my eyes on you."

A few days before our departure, Tim wanted to fish, so he asked Joe to bait his hook. Tim's eyes scanned the dark water slapping the *Elizabeth's* hull.

"Put a humungous chunk on it," he said. "I want to catch the big one."

We all knew who "the big one" was---an ancient fish who occasionally surfaced just long enough to tantalize us eager fishermen. Its big fin would appear out of nowhere; then its churning body would disappear before we could get a good look at it. Gale thought it might be a shark, but Joe and I guessed tarpon.

Joe was putting Tim's pole into a bracket on the stern end of the cockpit combing when Mom stuck her head out of the companionway.

"Where's Gale?" she asked. "It's time for lunch."

I knew where Gale was---out behind the fish company having a cigarette--- but I didn't say anything.

"She was here just a minute ago," Joe said.

Dad grabbed Walter's conch shell from its holder on the cabinside. He blew it loud three times, and a few minutes later, Gale came strolling home.

"Tuna or egg salad?" Mom asked.

"Tuna," Gale replied. "Do we have any pop?"

"Just this." Mom held her Tupperware pitcher in the air. "Half Coke and half ice tea. We can't afford to keep drinking Cokes. It's my own invention. "

We were just finishing our lunch when the line on Tim's reel started whizzing out.

"I got a bite! I got a bite!" He screamed.

Shocked to see his pole bent almost in half, I jumped up, but Tim was faster. Racing to the rod, he grabbed it out of the holder, but it almost pulled him off the boat. His feet were just starting to leave the deck when I grabbed him by the waist.

Ouch! Tim's face was all contorted, but he held tight to the pole. To stop the line from running out, he'd pressed down hard on the spinning coil with both thumbs. I could smell burning flesh.

"Give me the pole," I demanded. But, even though he had tears in his eyes, Tim wouldn't hand it over.

"No way, Jose!" He grunted. "This is my fish. I want to bring him in myself."

After almost an hour of playing the fish, along with some advice from a couple of fishermen who had come by to watch the action and much cheering by the family, Tim finally brought his prize alongside the boat.

"It's an alligator!" Joe shouted, but the fishermen on shore laughed.

"Nope. It's just a big old gar! Six feet at least. Y'all better be careful. That thing'll take an arm off. You better make a noose, not outta rope, but wire. It's the only way to bring that thing outta the water."

Dad shrugged. "I don't have any wire."

"Come on, Brett," the man said. "Let's go find some."

Gale and Tim leaped ashore to help. "We'll check the dumpster by the gate."

While he was waiting for the fishermen to come back, Dad hammered together a stand on shore. "Tim will want a picture of this one."

Joe and I stood watch over the big fish. At first it thrashed its tail around wildly, but eventually it stopped moving. Slowly it rolled over on its side, exposing a white underbelly.

When the fisherman came back, they made two nooses. One went over the fish's long ugly snout, the other around its belly. It took both fishermen and Dad to pull the monster from the water and lug it ashore.

After it was safely on the ground, Dad ran below to get a hatchet. "I'm going to make sure this fish is dead," he said.

Whack! Whack! Whack! Dad bent over the fish, hacking away at its leathery body. The hatchet just bounced off the fish's thick scales, but finally one of its fins came off.

"You folks oughta call the newspaper," one of the fishermen said. "Ain't every day a kid young as that lands such a big fish. Wouldn't surprise me one bit, if y'all broke some kind of record."

Mom grabbed Dad's arm. "Oh, yes! Call them Edward!"

When Dad came back from the fish company office, he was grinning. "They'll be here in a couple of hours," he said.

"Oh, boy!" Tim jumped up and down. "Oh, boy! I'll be in the newspaper. I'll be famous!"

All afternoon we sat in the hot sun watching the fish, but the reporters never came, and Timmy was horribly disappointed.

"I'm sorry, son," Dad said, "but I'm going to have to cut him down. It's almost high tide. If we throw him in now, he'll drift out to sea. If not, he'll rot here in the canal; a fish that big will stink to high heaven."

"Oh, Edward," Mom pleaded. "Can't we wait just a little while longer?"

We'd all pretty much given up hope, but a few minutes later the photographer came driving up in a big Buick. He posed Tim beside his fish and asked a lot of questions. When he was done, he poked Tim in the chest. "It'll be in Wednesday's paper. Sports section. Check it out, kid."

After the newspaper guy left, Dad and Joe dragged the fish over to the water's edge and kicked it into the murky out-going tide. Kerplunk!

For a minute the fish just floated there on its side, its head resting in a pile of foamy scum surrounded by a few empty wine bottles, a soggy six-pack beer carrier, and some bobbing wood-chips. It seemed like a sad way to go for a fish that had fought so hard. Like mourners at a funeral, we stood watching as the outgoing tide slowly pulled him away, but then Tim let out a scream.

"He's still alive!"

A shudder shook the fish's body. It tried to turn upright, but it couldn't get its balance. Its gills opened with a small hiss, but they only sucked air. His long snout with its rows of sharp tiny teeth gaped wide.

"Well, I'll be damned!" Dad shook his head.

"Come on! Come on! You can do it!" Tim shouted.

It took a few minutes, but finally the old fish arched his back and gathered enough strength to dive. We watched it work its way back into the safety of deeper water. Then it disappeared.

"He was such good fish." Tears glistened in Tim's eyes. "I'm glad he didn't die."

Mom and Tim posing on the bowsprit.

Chapter Seven

TWO HOURS OUT OF Pensacola, Dad called everyone on deck. The shoreline was a mere blur on the horizon. As she met the long off-shore waves, the *Elizabeth* hobby-horsed up and down. Joe, positioned at the foot of the mast, was ready for action.

"Okay, Joe, haul her up!" Dad shouted.

As the long edge of the sail rippled and chattered in the wind, we all looked skyward. Rust stains and brown mildew spots pockmarked its once white surface, but to us the sail full of wind was a beautiful thing to behold.

"Okay. Right there! Fasten that halyard to the cleat. I'm going to fall off the wind. Watch your heads!"

After Dad turned the motor off, the *Elizabeth* slowly heeled over, and white spray splashed over her rails. *Hip! Hip! Hooray!*

Dad's sunburned face broke into a big smile.

"This is it, Marie! Here we are under sail again. A good wife, great kids and a strong boat---what man could ask for anything more?"

Sailing offshore was different from being river-bound. If anything went wrong, we couldn't just drift to the nearest bank and go for help. We all knew the stories about boats being wrecked at sea. Falling overboard was a real danger, so for the first few days, we practiced lifesaving skills. We threw life jackets on ropes into the sea and then circled back to retrieve them. A few afternoon squalls brought dark clouds, torrential rain and strong winds, but Joe quickly learned how to handle the sails, and I was ready to jump the minute Dad gave an order. By the second day, we'd settled into an easy routine.

"This is really cool, Carole." Joe and I were sitting with our backs against the cabin-side, watching Tim troll a line off the stern. "Life is so simple out here. No bullshit. I don't think I've ever been this happy."

As we slowly skimmed along the coast of Florida's panhandle, our spirits were high. With salt-stained hair and clothes, we sat around the cockpit marveling at our good fortune.

"It's so quiet out here," Joe said.

Gale and I played cards with Tim or sat on the bowsprit watching the sandy bottom for coral or fish. Gale's feet dangled. Her hands grasped the forestay.

"I'm glad we moved on the boat, aren't you, Carole?"

"Sure," I said. "If we didn't, I never would have met Joe."

"You're so lucky."

"Don't worry. You'll meet somebody too."

"Not as handsome and fun as Joe."

"Maybe not." I laughed. "But he'll be perfect for you."

When night came, we took four hour watches. Standing in front of the glowing compass, holding the wheel in my hand, I felt the sea moving beneath me. Remembering all the early explorers that dared to sail across an ocean everyone said was flat, I admired their bravery. Looking up I thought--- those are the same stars.

When we finally reached the channel that led into Ft. Walton Beach, I changed into a cotton dress and walked to the end of the bowsprit, but a sudden drop in temperature, a cold front carrying Northern winds into the Gulf, forced me back into the cockpit where Joe was steering.

"I'm freezing," I said.

"Come sit by me." Joe patted the wheel-box next to him. When I sat down he put his arm around me.

The dock we found was blocks away from town, but a group of small buildings huddled at the end of the bridge that connected us to the shore.

"Look!" Joe said. "Over there. It's a BBQ shack. I can smell it!."

A stream of blue smoke curled into the sky over a pink pig-shaped building.

"Can we get some? Pleeease! " Tim moaned.

Dad handed Joe a couple of bills. "Sure. You kids deserve a treat. Let's celebrate. What does everyone want?"

I threw on a sweater, but walking across the bridge the wind tore at our clothes. A temperature sign on a yellow brick bank beside the BBQ said it was 55 degrees, but I had trouble believing it. Back in Chicago, 55 degrees was warm.

Hurrying into the warmth of the BBQ shack, I blew on my hands. Red and white checkered tablecloths, small pig-shaped sugar bowls, and napkins splattered with ears of corn, gave the place a cheerful look.

"Nasty wind, huh?" As the door slammed behind us, the clerk pulled her heavy, black sweater tighter. "The noon report said it's supposed to be seventy-five again tomorrow. I sure hope so. Not much business, when it's this cold."

After spending one night in Ft. Walton Beach, we headed for Panama City. The sun once again kissed the waves. We ate breakfast in the cockpit, read books, sang a few songs and took naps. Tim fished. Before we knew it, we were pulling into a brand new marina.

After taking a hot shower in the ultra-modern bathroom, I stood admiring my dark tan and sun-bleached hair in front of the mirror. Happy to be so clean and feeling full of love for my free life, I couldn't resist. Leaning forward, I kissed my mirror image full on the lips.

After supper, Tim and I were sitting on deck reading Archie comics. When Joe joined us, he put his hand on my leg. "Come on, Carole. Let's go for a walk."

"A walk? Where?" Tim asked. "Can I come too?"

"Nah, we might be gone a long time," Joe said.

Tim frowned. "I know why you want to be alone. You want to do all that mushy stuff."

"Yeah, the mushy stuff." Joe laughed.

"I'm going to tell."

"Aw, come on," Joe moaned.

"No. Really! Dad said to keep an eye on you two."

"Even if I give you my stainless steel pen?"

Tim's eyes opened wide. He no longer had to wear his little lifejacket, but he was always touching his chest as if it was still there.

"The one with the sailfish on it?"

"Yeah, it's the only one left, you little pirate. You already got all my other ones. "

Tim grinned. "Okay, it's a deal then. But you better not be gone long."

As we dropped our clothes on a nearby stretch of beach, a full moon rose. The warm Gulfstream water felt like silk against our skin. When we kissed, I licked Joe's salty lips. Off in the distance, the sound of Dad blowing his conch shell only added to the wild urgency of our lovemaking.

The next day, after a few hours of pleasant sailing, we cruised into Carrabelle, Florida. With its ancient buildings, picturesque waterfront and palm-lined roads, it looked like a 1930s postcard. The downtown was nothing more than a four-way stop, but the waterfront bustled with activity. Row after row of docks filled with commercial fishing boats with names like Princess Lulu and Lucky Strike jostled and bounced in the wake of a passing ferry. As we puttered up to the municipal dock, Mom pointed to some of the faded signs on the storefronts. Some of them were so old they advertised horseless carriages and Mrs. Winslow's Cough Syrup.

Dad chuckled. "Looks like they need a sign-painter here, Marie."

Joe and I barely had time to secure the dock lines when a man wearing a white shirt and tie came strolling over. "Howdy folks, y'all plan on staying long? I'm Wallace Short, the police chief here. It costs five dollars a night to tie up. Bathrooms are across the street. No showers. You pay me."

The Chief pulled a small, white Bull Durham sack from his pocket. He rolled a slim cigarette and slid his tongue over it.

Dad smiled. "Well, actually, I was hoping to stay a few months," he said. "We're heading to St. Pete. I'm a sign painter, so

I was hoping to get some work here. I notice you don't have a dock sign. How about letting me paint one in exchange for the dock fees?"

"That'd be fine by me." The police chief nodded his head toward town. "But I don't imagine you'll have much luck getting work. A few years back, a sign painter came through here. Big talker, that one was. Painted four or five big window signs, then high-tailed it out of town. I don't know what kind of paint he used, but the first time it rained, all the signs washed away. I tried tracking him down, but he'd run off to Georgia. Not my jurisdiction."

Dad pulled a business card from his wallet. "Well, I'm a professional," he said. "I had my own outdoor advertising business in Chicago. I stand behind what I do."

Carrabelle's fishing boats were high in the bow and low in the stern. They looked like sailboats, but they only had one short mast for a steadying sail and each had a small wheelhouse on the stern. The boats traveled all the way to Mexico, to the Banks of Capeche, to fish for snapper and grouper.

Within weeks of our arrival, we knew everyone in town. The fishermen found us fascinating. They admired Dad for daring to leave the rat-race behind. Escaping forever, to an island like Tahiti, seemed practical to them, so they embraced us. Every day one of the big commercial boats drew alongside the *Elizabeth* to drop off a huge snapper or a coal sack of oysters.

Across from us, a noisy processing plant clanged with activity. Incoming boats unloaded their catches. Outgoing ones took on ice and gas. All day trucks zoomed back and forth carrying the fresh catch to customers all across the South.

The one store in town, a general store owned by the fish company, was a real "company store" like the one in the Ernie Ford song. Its shadowy interior held row after row of shelves offering everything from canned food to yard goods. Barrels and bins stocked with fishing gear and hardware littered the worn wooden floor. All the fishermen shopped there because it was easy to get credit, but the prices were highly inflated and their wages extremely low, so no one ever got caught up.

Dad did find work, but the police chief turned out to be right. It took a long time for people to trust anyone who professed to be sign painter.

One day when we were having lunch at Harry the Greek's Restaurant, Harry stopped by our table.

"Is everything okay?"

"Delicious," Mom said. "Especially the salad. It was so big, I could hardly finish it."

When Dad asked for the bill, Harry told the waitress not to charge for dessert.

"It's on me," he said. "You got a nice family there. Welcome to Carrabelle."

"Thank you! That's very nice of you. By the way, I'm a sign painter. Would you be interested in a new sign? I couldn't help but notice that yours is faded."

Harry shifted the toothpick in his mouth back and forth.

"Well, I don't know."

"I'm very professional," Dad said. "I stand behind every job. Advertising is very cost effective. Anybody passing through here is going to stop at the place with the nicest sign."

Harry looked wistful. "I'd like to have one, but business has been pretty slow lately. Cash is hard to come by. I might consider bartering some meals though. "

After thinking it over, Dad agreed. "Okay, I'll start tomorrow."

The minute the other businessmen in town saw how nice Harry's new sign looked, they all wanted one. None of them had any money either, so before we knew it, we had tabs everywhere.

At Budha's Pharmacy, we charged nickel cokes. At Essie Mae's Korner Kitchen Kafe, it was fried pies and meatloaf dinners. We even had a tab at the local movie theatre, a dilapidated barn of a place that looked like it had been built in the Civil War days. Most of the films were B movies, and they only had one showing a week. If you came in late, the man that ran the projector knew it. Out of courtesy, he would run the movie just to the point where you came in. Sometimes right in the middle of a sentence, the actors' voices would start to drag. Then, the film would start flipping. Before you knew, it the screen went blank.

Every morning Dad marched into town carrying his sign kit. Mostly he worked alone, but sometimes Joe helped him. Lonely without Joe, I carried my sketchbook down to the waterfront or fished for crabs. All I had to do was tie a string around a chicken back and dip it in the water. I could feel the line throb when the scuttling crabs climbed aboard. When I yanked my bait up, the chicken back would be crawling with snapping pincers and waving antennas. Robbie, a fisherman on the Miss Nancy showed me how to press my finger hard against their shells to avoid their scissor sharp claws. Gingerly throwing them into a pail, I'd bring them home for Mom to make crab cakes. Occasionally I walked into town to see if I could spy Joe and Dad at work.

One day I passed an old store with a wooden front porch: Lester Busby's Sundry Shop. An old Coke sign nailed to the wall beside the door looked inviting so I stepped in. The store was huge, but empty. A double row of ceiling fans twirled over my head.

"What can I getcha?"

Lester, a curly-haired man who never spoke much, sat on a high stool perched behind a long wooden counter. The shelves behind him were empty except for one box of shoe laces and some yellowed notebook paper.

"A Coke, please."

Choosing one of the empty tables I sat down. The whole place looked like an antique store, so I was fascinated by the embossed metal ceiling tiles, the old jukebox, and the row of pinball machines along one wall. Feeling around in my pocket, I found a dime, so I decided to play. The baseball machine sported a smooth green field with bleachers full of cheering people. After I inserted my dime in the steel slider, I pushed it forward, and the machine came alive. Pulling the metal plunger as far back as I could, I let her rip, and the steel ball at the end of the row went shooting into a maze of plastic circles, bumpers and flippers set on a baseball diamond. When I hit a home run, a metal guy ran the bases. A plaque under the glass said I'd get a free game if I could score 500, so I concentrated harder. When my little steel ball threatened to disappear into one of the holes, I grabbed the machine with both hands. I shoved my hip against one side. Here, there, across the glass top, down the center, by that time I was addicted. All I could think of was getting another dime, so I could play again. Eventually I got so good I could win free games every time, but there were those days when even a dime was hard to come by.

When I wasn't hovering over the pinball machine, I joined a group of fishermen who spent every day sitting on wire milk-crates in the weedy lot next to Lester's. Most of their talk revolved around who caught how much and where, what kind of storms they'd met, whose girlfriend was cheating, or whose kid was in jail. Barefoot Benny and Punkin' Head teased me like jovial uncles, but they also taught me how to roll cigarettes. They warned me not to whistle at sea for fear of "whistling up the wind", and they also taught me a lot about fishing, which fish were bottom feeders, which ones you had to troll for. They said patience helped set a hook just right. You had to get past the nibble and wait until the whole thing was swallowed.

"There's an art to it," Benny said. "After a while your fingers know everything."

Sometimes it was hard to tell if the yarns the men told were true. Master storytellers every one, their stores included everything from jail breaks to close encounters with enraged husbands. Pinky Brown bragged that he'd eaten human flesh or "long pig" as he called it, and Silly Gilly swore he'd been married to the daughter of the President of Cuba two times. Barefoot Benny was a born flirt and the resident expert on romance. He'd been married five times, so the others looked to him for advice about women. One day when a young kid was moaning about losing his pretty girl to a man on another boat, Benny shook his head. "Don't ever marry a good lookin' woman," he said. "My third wife was a looker. Ran off with a shoe salesman from Tennessee. Getcha an ugly one, sos nobody else is gonna want 'er. When the lights go out, won't make one bit a difference. Older ladies are grateful for anything they can get and most of 'em can cook real good too. You marry a woman you love. That's trouble for sure."

I felt sorry for Punkin'Head. A gentle man with a limp and a head the size of a watermelon, he wasn't the sharpest knife in the drawer, but he had been a merchant seaman out of New York at one time. He traveled the world, but lost his seaman's license because he'd started a fire. Alcohol on boats is always taboo in the crew's quarters, but Punkin'Head stashed a flask under his bunk. One night he got drunk and fell asleep with a cigarette in his mouth. By the time he woke up, the whole cabin was on fire. Every time Punkin' Head saw me, his face lighted up. "Howdy, Miss Carole. The Good Lord surely is shinin' down on Carrabelle today. Got me a letter from Momma."

At first, I just listened to the tinkling rhythms of the fishermen's talk, but after a while I wanted to make them laugh at my stories too, so I started telling them about our adventures on the river. Holding their attention wasn't easy. Competition came from all sides, and the worst sin you could commit was to be boring. Eventually, I learned to embellish things a little. Then I learned to embellish them a whole lot.

One hard-ass fisherman named Catfish always got nervous around me. Hardly a sentence came out of his mouth that didn't contain a curse word or two. Considering myself to just be one of the guys, I didn't mind, but lanky old Catfish wasn't used to having a girl around. "Couldn't catch a fish for two days," he'd say. "But then we hit such a fuckin' (excuse me Ma'am) big school we hardly had time to haul em up and put more bait on. Those bastards (sorry, Ma'am) practically jumped into the boat. Coming home our rail was only a couple of inches from the water. Shit! (excuse me, Ma'am) We got almost $35 dollars a share!"

That's how the fishermen got paid. After every trip, they divvied up the profits. The captain got the biggest share, and the boat got one too, then the crew. A hundred dollar trip was unheard of, but all the fishermen dreamed of someday having one.

When I ran out of bait money or couldn't get a dime for the pinball machine, I'd wander over to the Korner Kitchen Kafe. With her red hair bobbing and long earrings swinging, Essie Mae poured coffee and served up advice to her regular customers. Some of the fisherman had wives, and they counted on Essie Mae's wagging tongue. "I saw his car parked a block away from her house all night," she'd say. "If Luella knew he was foolin' with a skag like that, she'd cut his balls off."

Essie liked me a lot, so sometimes she let me hang around after the café closed. One day she shocked me, by asking if Joe and I used rubbers. "Them sperms are strong," she said. "You gotta inspect every one. Some people prick 'em with pins, ya know. Think they're bein' funny. You're too young to get knocked up. Get yourself an education. Nothing worse than having to beg a man for spending money."

Every paradise has to have a flaw. In Carrabelle, tiny gnats called no-see-ums drove us crazy the whole time we were there. It seemed impossible that anything that small would be capable of such a painful sting, but the Carrabelle gnats made even a wasp bite seem like child's play. When they stung you, it felt like fire had been injected into one of your nerves. Most of the locals seemed to have become immune to them, but we suffered horribly. Within weeks, our legs were dotted with red, ulcerated sores that took weeks to heal.

When Joe didn't have to help Dad, we went fishing. For a nickel, we could buy a mullet. Punkin' Head had taught me how to slit its belly, slide a hook inside, and then sew it up again. "If you wanna catch a big fish, you gotta use big bait. Same goes for life."

When the inky-black nights came, we gigged with flashlights for flounders in the Crooked River. The flat fish burrowed down in the sandy bottom, so they were hard to see, but the minute you got close to one, it would flutter up and zoom away. Wearing sneakers, wading through the shallow river water, Gale and I hated the way the tiny needle-fish nibbled the hair on our bare legs, but Tim didn't care. Every time we went gigging, he insisted on coming along.

One night when Joe was a few steps ahead of us, Tim grabbed my arm and held me back. Shining his flashlight in my face, he was jittery with excitement.

"Joe's making you a surprise," he said.

"Well, what is it?" I asked.

"I can't tell you." Tim grinned. "But, you sure are going to like it!"

Now some people might not think getting a gig from your boyfriend was the most exciting thing that could happen to a girl, but for me it might as well have been a diamond.

"I made it out of a broomstick and a nail." Joe held the gig in striking position. "I know how much you like those Turk's Head knots. I used wax string, so it won't matter if it gets wet."

Mom favorite entertainment was a visit to the abandoned ante-bellum house that sat on a high bluff overlooking the harbor. The once elegant plantation-style home with its sweeping veranda, wood columns, high-ceilinged rooms and widow's walk, obviously had been built by someone who had a lot of money and a love for the sea. "What a shame," Mom said.

One day we brought a picnic lunch up there, and Mom let her imagination soar with the sea gulls. "Don't you think this place would make a great restaurant?" she asked. "I bet if someone fixed this place up, they could make a bundle of money. If I owned a place like this, that's what I'd do. Just look at this view! I'd serve gourmet food and put a row of tables on the porch. People from all over the South would come."

"It could also be a hotel." Gale waved her bologna sandwich toward the weedy overgrown lawn. "The first thing I'd do is plant one of those big flower gardens like we saw on the plantations. You could put fresh roses on all the tables and in the rooms too. Hey! Maybe we could call it *The Rose House Inn*!"

Mom refilled my Wyler's lemonade glass. "Or Hawaiian orchids. I think white orchids on every table would be nice. Especially at night."

"I'd mount a telescope on the porch." I said.

"Gee, what a great idea, Carole! You know Dad promised to buy me a house after Tahiti. I doubt if he'll ever give up sailing though. If I had a place like this, he could be gone as much as he wants. In the morning I'd put on a Japanese kimono and have coffee on the porch. I'd install a big Chinese gong on the lawn.

That way, when I saw his boat coming in, I could run down and ring it."

Walking across the porch to peer through the broken glass panes that ran along both sides of the stately front door, Gale swatted a gnat on her leg. "What kind of furniture would we have?"

"Southern, of course." Mom wiped her forehead with a paper napkin. "Gas lamps with handpainted globes and big old four-poster beds with embroidered, white coverlets. I'd put blue velvet chairs and floor-to-ceiling bookcases in the parlor. Our guests would probably like to read. We might even arrange intimate little discussions groups about books in the evening."

"And costume-parties!" Gale giggled. "We could all wear hoop skirts and wigs! We could hire an orchestra. Everyone could dance on the lawn."

By the time Christmas rolled around, Dad was broke. He'd painted just about every sign in town, but everything was bartered. "It's going to be a pretty gloomy Christmas." Mom sighed. Joe, however, had other ideas. One day he and Tim dragged home a scraggly pine tree they'd liberated from a small weedy area behind Lester's shop. The two of them were in great spirits as they mounted it on the main cabin-top. That afternoon,

I cut out a few tin foil stars and made a garland of popcorn. Gale retrieved some tin-can tops from the dumpster behind Harry's. She punched a hole in each one and dangled them from the tree's bristling branches with paper clips. "Who needs lights?"

A few minutes later, Tim ran to get a box of construction paper and a pair of scissors. Grabbing a stack of magazine, he cut out gifts for everyone--- a pair of new oars for Dad, a sports car for Joe, an Elvis record for Gale.

After that, we all took turns. I found a big Chinese gong for Mom. Gale gave her an English tea pot. On the upper branches of the tiny tree, Dad hung a pair of roller skates for Gale and a Pflueger Rocket fishing reel for Joe. Mom gave Dad a Danforth anchor, a Swiss Army knife, and a hundred-dollar bill. "It's just pretend." She laughed. "So why not go all the way?"

When Christmas Day came, we didn't have money enough to buy a turkey or ham. We could have had fish, but by that time we were sick of fish. Snapper stew, fried grouper, flounder over spaghetti. Mom did her best, but after a while, it got pretty boring. Instead she made buttered spaghetti with real butter. After we ate dinner, the family gathered on deck. Holding hands, we circled the tree and sang carols. *Silent Night, Come All Ye Faithful, and Little Town of Bethlehem.* Under the starry sky, a white moon rose to gild all our trinkets with silver light. I had to blink hard to hold back the tears.

As the months drifted by we got so comfortable in Carrabelle, time once again forgot us. Life was good, and Dad got a lot of work done on the boat, but when summer came, it was too hot to do much, so all we did was swim, fish, and swap stories with the locals.

"When are we going to get out of here?" Mom asked.

"I'm working on that, Marie. We still need more money. I need to find somebody with cash." Dad wiped the sweat off his chest with a rag and frowned, but a few days later, he headed over to Apalachicola, a small town just down the highway to look for more work.

Bus service was limited, so like everyone else in town, he rode over to Apalach with Judge Witherspoon. All you had to was show up. Every morning at exactly eight-thirty, the Judge would pop out of his house and everyone would climb into his wood-paneled station wagon. When four o'clock came, they gathered on the courthouse steps. There was no set time for the return trip. Some days Judge Witherspoon heard more cases than others.

Because Mom's usually cheerful attitude was dropping like a barometer before a big storm, I decided to help out. Money was our only problem, so I went looking for a waitress job. No one needed a waitress, but one day I saw a COOK WANTED sign in a small seafood restaurant. I didn't have any cooking experience, but figured I could learn, and lucky for me, I got hired right away.

Standing in front of a big stainless steel grill, peering into the dining area through a little kitchen window, waves of anxiety washed over me. I'd gone over the menu with Mom, so I had a pretty good idea how to make most of the dishes they offered, but I still needed to learn the routine. I expected the waitresses to like me because I'd been a waitress too. Penny, a pretty blond with big round eyes, was my age. Kristy had three boys, and Doris had a cat named Felix. The boss, a guy named T-Bone, was nice enough, but a few minutes after we opened, he said he had to leave. "Sorry, but I've got some business in town. The girls will show you the ropes."

After he left, Penny snorted. "Yeah, monkey business."

As I watched the waitresses race around to take orders, I felt a lump in my throat. How could I do this all alone? Just the smell of the place made me want to throw up. I kept picturing myself sprinting out the front door, but there simply wasn't time.

The first few orders were easy, just soup or hamburgers and fries, but then Penny handed me a ticket full of seafood orders. "I need five snapper plates," she grinned. "The people are in a hurry, so maybe you could put a rush on it?"

Hurrying into the back room, I opened the refrigerator, but no matter how much I shoved things around, I couldn't find anything marked snapper. The dishwasher, a guy named Domino, leaned against a double sink, twirling a Q-tip in his ear. Holding up a white bucket marked FISH, I asked him, "Is this the snapper?"

"Yup," he said.

By the time I got back to the cook's station, a thick pile of tickets bristled on my spindle: a hamburger—rare with no onions; three catfish dinners; two snapper dinners, a fisherman's platter, four separate hot dogs and three steaks. Whipping the hamburger patty, hotdogs, and steaks onto the grill, I raced back to the fridge.

"Were do they keep the catfish?" I panted.

When Domino smiled his tobacco-stained gums looked black. His tongue moved in and out of his mouth like a lizard. "Same place as the snapper." He grinned.

"You're kidding?"

"No, I ain't kidding. Most people come in here can't tell snapper from catfish. Georgia crackers mostly. Dumb as boards. Makes no sense for T-Bone to pay a fortune. All the fishes on the menu, no matter what you call em, they all come from that same big ol' tub."

Feeling guilty, I grabbed a handful of the fish, along with a big pan of shrimp, crabs and hushpuppies.

Kristy shoved her pencil behind her ear. "Hey, you got my seafood platters yet?"

"In a minute," I said. "I had trouble finding the fish."

"In a minute?" Kristy groaned. "These people have to catch a charter. They've already been here twenty-five minutes."

"Gee, I'm sorry." I shrugged. "I did tell T-bone I never cooked before."

Kristy pushed her hands deep into her apron pockets. Her lower lip jutted out so far it almost touched her nose. "Shoot! There go my tips."

Watching her stomp away, I wanted to throw something at her.

When I finally got back to the boat, Mom and Joe were sitting on deck. Peering over her glasses, Mom asked, "So how was it, Carole?"

Joe pulled me onto his lap. "Was it busy?"

"It was horrible!" I whined. "They advertise snapper, but it's all catfish. Everything's catfish! I'm not going back."

The morning after my restaurant fiasco, Joe said he was determined to get a job on one of the fishing boats. "I hear Capt. Massey on the Lucky Strike is hiring. Your dad shouldn't have to support us."

"Show me yur hands." That's all Captain Algae Massey said when Joe applied for the job. Once he saw Joe's calloused palms, he nodded. "Bring a pair of oilskins and boots. If yuh ain't got any, the boat's got an account at the store. Whatcha buy'll come out of your share."

That night, after supper, Dad made Joe feel like a hero. Banging his fork against his coffee cup, he asked for everyone's attention. "Listen up," he said. "As you already know, Joe has offered to go fishing. It will be a long and dangerous trip, so he deserves a lot of credit." Dad put his hand on Joe's shoulder. "I know I've called you a nincompoop many times, Joe, but I'm taking that back. Today, I am officially promoting you to nincom. If you work real hard, you could even become a nin. We'll have to see after that, but I want you to know, we all really do appreciate your pitching in."

"Three cheers for Joe!" Tim shouted, and we all joined in. "Hip hip hooray! Hip hip hooray for Joe!"

From the moment Joe left until the day he came home, I suffered a loneliness I'd never felt before. Up until that time, the family was the center of my world, but now my allegiance had shifted. Joe was my whole world now. He was my future, and I couldn't imagine life without him. Thoughts about him being so far away, facing high seas and only God knew what else, pestered my mind. What if he died out there? What if he never came back? Sometimes I would climb up to the old house on the bluff, to stand on the porch overlooking the sea. Up there, I felt a kinship with all the women whose husbands or lovers were fishermen, and all the generations of women before us who were forced to scan the distant horizon, hoping to see a boat they recognized, hoping their men would come home from the sea without a missing finger or a hook in the eye.

One afternoon, I was playing pinball at Lester's, when a fisherman named One Eyed Jack came rushing through the door. "They's back, Ma'am!" He jerked his thumb toward the docks. "Capt. Randy jus picked 'em up on the radio."

It wasn't considered proper for women to go running down to the docks when a boat came in, so I ran home instead.

"It'll take a while before he gets here," Dad said. "They'll have to unload the fish first and clean up the boat."

"Well, I sure hope he's hungry," Mom said. "Benny dropped off a whole bucket of shrimp this afternoon. I'm making jambalaya."

The minute I saw Joe coming down the dock, I ran to greet him. He carried a forty-pound grouper in one hand and his rucksack in the other. Grabbing the rucksack, I kissed him hard. "Everyone is waiting to hear how your trip went."

After he'd washed up, Joe lifted the lid from Mom's jambalaya.

"Smells good, Marie," he said. "Nothing like home cooking."

After dinner Mom cleared away the plates. "Should I serve dessert now?"

"No!" Tim said. "We want to hear Joe's stories first!"

"Well, I hated it at first. Most of the fishermen are winos, so the first few days out, everybody was puking and getting the shakes. Some guys were hallucinating. I'd never seen anything like that before. The cook kept hosing the foc'sle down using Pinesol to get rid of the vomit smell. That stuff was disgusting ! On the other hand, it was beautiful. Man, you should have seen the color of the water. It was crazy beautiful. Once we reached the fishing grounds, we got a rhythm going. Sun-up to sundown, we hauled them in. After supper, we'd sit around yakking for a while, usually, about women or the catch. Romeo, a kid from Texas played concertina. He showed me how to work it. Being a snapper fisherman is hard, but being out to sea that long is a great experience. I can't imagine anything better." Joe put his hand on my knee and squeezed it. "Except being here with my girl, of course."

"I want to be a fisherman!" Tim moaned.

"No, you don't. They use old tricycle wheels and car-springs for tackle. Every line has three hooks on it. Snappers and groupers can weigh 20 pounds, and you've got to crank them up by hand, a hundred feet, sometimes more. Once you get them to the rail, you have to jam your hand in their gills to pull them on board. Those gills have poison in them." Joe showed us his bruised and swollen hands. "See that? The captain said to soak them in Lysol. It'll draw all that stuff out."

"Did you run into any storms?" Gale asked.

"A few, but we couldn't fish in heavy weather, so I didn't mind. Those old guys are strong. After a couple of days, my body got used to it, but the first week out, I couldn't wait for heavy seas and rain. "

"Did you catch a lot of fish?" Mom asked.

Joe shrugged and lit a cigarette. "My share was twenty dollars, but I had to buy oilskins, so I only ended up with fifteen."

The next day, Joe offered to buy me breakfast at Essie Mae's. "You can order whatever you want," he said.

Walking through town, I felt dizzy. The sun beating down on my head felt extra hot. Heat mirages floated above the asphalt street. We were almost to the restaurant, when my foot slipped sideways, and I almost fell. Joe grabbed me by the waist and chuckled. "Hey! Have you been drinking?"

I slapped his shoulder. "No, I'm just dizzy in love with you," I said.

After saying hello and chatting a bit with everyone we knew, we slipped into a booth. While Joe was reading the menu, I started flipping through the pages of songs on the tiny chrome jukebox at the end of our table. I'd just selected a Nat King Cole song when I felt my stomach cramp and everything went blurry. I moved closer to Joe, so I could lay my head on his shoulder.

"Are you okay?" he asked.

"No. I'm having cramps. I think I need to go to the bathroom."

Slamming my hands against the door with the mermaid sign, I headed straight for the stalls. I didn't throw up, but I couldn't stop gagging.

When I came back, Joe looked worried.

"It's just the excitement," I said. "You got no idea how much I missed you. I'm so glad you're back."

Joe lifted my hand to his lips. "I missed you too, Carole. A whole lot."

It didn't take very long for me to realize I was pregnant. Every time I tried to eat something, it came right up. Because my daily diet consisted mostly of barbeque potato chips and strawberry pop, I left a trail of pink puke everywhere I went. Not exactly a cause for celebration. I believed Joe would someday ask me to marry him, but down the road, not now, not while we were still traveling, and my parents would of course be livid. The words *shotgun wedding* haunted me, so for a few weeks I didn't say anything. If anyone asked what was wrong, I blamed it on the flu. One night when Joe and I were walking along the waterfront, the oily combination of fresh caught fish and muddy sea bottom made my stomach churn. I burst into tears.

"What's wrong? Maybe you should see a doctor, Carole."

Sitting down on a dock-box in front of the *Miss Eleanor*, I had to tell him. "I'm pregnant, Joe. I'm so sorry, but don't feel like you have to marry me." Swiping the back of my hand under my nose, I took a deep breath. "If I have to, I can have this baby alone."

Joe held me until I stopped crying, then he placed his hand on my belly. "A baby? Really?"

When I saw the corners of his mouth lift in a smile, my upside- down world turned right-side up again. Pretty soon, we were both laughing.

"Of course, I'll marry you!" he said. "Don't be silly. That was the plan all along, but not now, after we get to Saint Pete. A marriage license costs money, and we'll need to get an apartment."

"I hadn't thought about that. Moving off the boat and all. What will Mom and Dad do? What about our trip? They won't be able to handle the boat alone."

"Well, there won't be room for us all on the boat, but don't worry, your parents will figure something out. They still have Gale, and Timmy can help. You can't stay home forever. You have your own life, your own dreams to follow---our dreams. Maybe we'll buy a boat someday. Start a charter business. Take people

out for daytrips. You, me and the baby. Wouldn't that be fun?"
Joe put his hand on my belly. "As soon as we get to St. Pete," he
said. "I'll get a job, Carole. We'll get married, but I don't think we
should tell your parents right now."

"I don't either." I agreed. "Once we're there, we can both get
jobs. If we can support ourselves, it will be a lot easier."

Just when our financial situation looked most desperate,
Dad got a lucky break. Noah Snow the owner of the only motel
in Carrabelle and the richest man in town asked him to build a
billboard sign. He offered free rent at his dock while we worked
on it, and he could pay cash.

"Oh, boy! Big bucks!" Dad grabbed Mom by the waist and
swung her around. "This will give us enough to head for St. Pete,
but I have to say, I hate leaving this place. A few more years and
little fishing towns like this will no long exist."

Mom raised an eyebrow. One hip tilted toward him. "Not
me," she said. "I'm looking forward to getting to St. Pete. I hope
we can stay there awhile, too. We really have to get these kids in
school, Edward. This trip is taking a lot longer than I thought."

Joe worked digging holes for the big sign. When Dad
asked me to draw the six-foot tall diving girl to be mounted on
the top, I felt honored.

Unfurling a roll of brown paper on the dock, he said. "It'll be easy. I'll make a grid. I'm sure we can find a picture of a diving girl somewhere. I'll use a blow-up machine. All you'll have to do is copy it, square by square."

After we transferred my drawing to a big sheet of plywood, I couldn't believe how good she looked. Dad only had a small keyhole saw, so it was taking him forever to cut her out.

One afternoon a big bear of a man with a long grey ponytail wandered onto the dock.

"What yuh need is a saber saw."

A long stream of tobacco fell close to my bare toes.

"I know." Dad grunted. "But I don't have one."

"I'll letcha borry mine," the man said.

"No, thanks." Dad smiled. "That's okay. I hate borrowing things. Especially tools."

"Shoot. You'll be there a month of Sundays, if yuh don't."

After watching a few more minutes, the man walked away. When he came back, he had his electric saber saw in one hand. "Here." He pushed it toward Dad. "Jes try it. You'll see."

Not wanting to offend the guy, Dad took the saw, but before he could use it, Mom's head popped out of the companionway hatch. "Lunch time! Come and get it."

"Would you like to join us?" Dad asked.

"Naw, cain't. The man smiled. "Got to go to Apalach today to deliver a sink. Junks my business. Used sinks, terlits, bathtubs, any kinda plumbin' stuff. Yuh kin keep the saw. I'll git it tomorrow."

"Well...okay," Dad said. "Thanks."

After lunch, I sat on the opposite end of the sheet of plywood to stop it from bouncing. Dad slid the saw blade into a cut along the diving girl's shoulder and pushed down. He'd only moved it an inch or two when the blade suddenly broke. "Damn it!" Dad groaned. "See why I hate borrowing things? Now I'll have to buy this guy a brand new blade."

The next morning, after Dad left for Apalachicola, Tim and I fished off the boat. The morning sun was hot, but by afternoon it was scorching. When Dad came back, he was in a bad mood. "Thank god, I found this. It's the last blade in town." Sweat dripped down his forehead, but he threw his shirt off and went right to work. A few minutes later, just before he got to the diving girl's neck, I heard a sharp clink, and the saw stopped.

"Dammit!" Dad sputtered. "How can that be? Something is wrong with this saw. I'll just give it back to him."

In the morning, when the man returned, Dad handed him his tool. "Thanks, but I'd rather use my own saw. Yours keeps breaking blades. I bought you a new one yesterday, but it broke too. Something is wrong with your saw."

"Ain't nothing wrong with that saw."

Dad shrugged. "It breaks new blades every time."

"Well, shit," the man said. "What am I supposed to do now?"

"Send it back to the factory, I guess."

After the man stomped off, Dad looked worried. "I don't trust that guy," he said. "Maybe he knew the saw was broken. I thought it was kind of fishy, the way he forced that thing on me."

In spite of how hard it was to cut the diving-girl out by hand, Dad, spurred on by anger, finished the job quickly. When the sign was done the whole family gathered to admire its glorious size.

The next day, when Mr. Snow came to pay Dad, he brought some bad news. "A hurricane is brewing in the Gulf. It could be here early as tonight. You might want to consider taking your boat up the river."

"What river are they talking about?" Mom said.

"It doesn't matter, Marie. With our depth, we won't be able to follow them. Right now, I'm going to hitchhike to the bank in Apalach to cash this check. If we do have to move the boat, I need to get the motor going. I started tearing it down last week to fix one of the valves. I need a couple of parts."

It didn't take Dad long to get a ride. The minute he got to the main road and put his thumb out, a truck stopped. "I'm not going all the way into town," the man said. "Just to my sister-in-law's place down the road, but it shouldn't take long for you to get another ride. Even if you don't, you can walk it. I've done it plenty of times."

As they rode the ribbon of highway, the man said he'd just moved there from Michigan.

"I like it here. No snow."

"It's a perfect place to live aboard a boat." Dad grinned.

"Not much work though."

"No. If there was, we'd probably stay here longer."

"Where you headed?"

"Tahiti, hopefully. It's always been my dream to sail there."

"Where's that?"

"A long way away," Dad said. "5,000 miles past the Panama Canal."

"How long will it take you?"

"I don't know." Dad shrugged. "And I don't care really."

The man shook his head. "Hey, I like your attitude! When I was younger, I used to think about buying a boat, but my wife wouldn't go for it. We live with my in-laws right now. It's not easy."

Dad rubbed his hands on his knees. "Marie is a good sport. Well, most of the time anyway. She wanted to buy a house. I talked her into this, but she is enjoying the trip. She's a history buff. Being on the Mississippi River was like going back in time. You see everything when you're traveling. I couldn't ask for a better wife. "

When the man pulled off the road, he pointed to a stand of tall palm trees. "Wait over there. It'll be a lot cooler."

Dad slammed the car door shut. "Thanks!"

Looking both ways, Dad didn't see any cars, so he started walking. Heat painted puddles of sky in the hot asphalt. A snapping turtle sat perched on a log, its head out, enjoying the sun. Right behind it, a white crane stalked through a clump of sawgrass. Dad was wondering if the turtle would sense the bird, when he heard the sound of a car coming. At first he thought the battered old Ford wasn't going to stop, but it did. Forty feet ahead of him the brakes squealed and a swirl of dust rose. As he ran towards it, a skinny woman in a wrinkled dress hopped out of the car. Without even looking at him, she scurried around to the back and climbed in.

Panting from the long run, Dad approached the car.

"Git in," the man said.

It only took Dad a minute to realize it was the guy with the saw, but by that time, it was already too late.

"Git in," the man repeated. So Dad did.

Bouncing up and down on a trash-littered front seat, trying to fit his feet around rusted pipes and toilet parts, Dad smelled whiskey. Looking over his shoulder at the woman crouched in the back seat, he gave her a weak smile, but she didn't smile back.

When the car swerved off the highway onto a gravel road, Dad frowned. "Hey, I'm going to Apalachicola," he said.

"We're takin' a short-cut."

A few yards later, the trees thickened and high weeds brushed against the car. When the driver suddenly hit the brakes, Dad's chin hit his chest. When his head came up again, he saw the guy had a knife. He started to say, "Hey, come on…" but, the long hunting knife was already pushing against his throat.

"Yuh damn Yankees." Hatred lighted a fire in the man's hard-jawed face. "Yuh come down here in yur fancy yachts. Think yur shit don't stink, but yuh broke my saw."

"I bought you a new blade." Dad protested.

"You broke my damn saw!"

"Cut 'im , Abner. Cut 'im!" The woman in the back seat bounced up and down.

When the guy turned half-around to tell her to shut-up, Dad grabbed the door handle. There was a tussle, but he somehow managed to shove the man's arm away. Leaping out, Dad ran back to the highway. When he saw a nearby house, he sprinted toward it. He'd almost made it to the driveway when the old Ford came squealing up behind him. Cutting across the front lawn, Dad ran for the front porch, but the car followed. Big clumps of grass and dirt flew through the air. He'd almost made it to the steps, when the owner came out carrying a shotgun. He had to fire twice in the air before the Ford took off.

"That nut tried to kill me," Dad said. "Can I use your phone?"

"Won't do a lick a good. That was Abner McFeeney chasin' yuh. If he wants to kill yuh, then no police is goin' to stop im."

He's already killed three men, I know of. Never spent a day in jail, either."

"You've got to be kidding," Dad said.

"No. I ain't. He'll sneak up on you when no one's around. Then... " The man made a quick slicing motion across his neck. "Say, where yuh live? I'd be glad to carry you home."

"I was on my way to the bank in Apalachicola."

"Well, that's okay, I'll take yuh there. Then, drive yuh home."

Mom was playing cards with Timmy, when Dad come scrambling down the companionway ladder. His hands were shaking, and there was a wild look in his eye.

Mom gasped "What is it, Edward?"

"That son of a bitch with the saw tried to kill me!" Dad rubbed his neck. "I've got to get the motor going. Hurricane or no hurricane, we've got to get out of here. It'll be safer at sea anyway. We're too deep to go up the river."

Mom frowned. She folded her cards with a snap.

"Land is the enemy in a storm, Marie. The *Elizabeth* is built for heavy weather. It's either that or end up in someone's backyard. Once this thing hits, boats will be flying all around."

As news of our plight reached the fishing docks, several of our fishermen friends came to help.

"Taint fair!" Bennie said. "Abner ain't got no right messing with yuns. Yur good people."

By the time the motor was running again, a parade of fishing boats streamed past the *Elizabeth* on their way inland. One of the captains shouted. "Better get movin'. She's gonna be here in a couple hours."

Dad yelled back. "Too deep, we're headed out to sea."

By nightfall the leading edge of the storm could be felt. The sky blackened and everything fell silent. Stoplights and neon signs glowed with other-worldly light.

"This could get exciting!" Joe said.

As the *Elizabeth* headed out of the harbor, the wind picked up and rain started. Slow at first, then harder and harder. Boney fingers of lightening illuminated the horizon. Out in the bay, the dark shape of Dog Island was being swallowed by waves and flying water.

"Go below, Carole," Dad said. "Make sure your Mom's okay. Bring me the chart on the table."

As I made my way down the companionway ladder, the boat rocked violently from side to side.

"Is that you, Edward?" Mom shouted from her bunk.

"No, it's me."

Gale's legs swiveled with the boat's churning motion. The washcloth she held on Mom's forehead smelled sour.

"It's awfully rough," Mom said. "I hear cracking noises."

"It is," I said. "But, we're fine. As soon as we get behind the island, it'll calm down."

"I want to be on deck!" Tim whined.

"Hush!" Mom said. "It's too rough. I need you and Gale here with me."

By the time I got back to the cockpit, waves were crashing over our bow. Mountain-sized swells loomed all around us. When I peered out to sea, the wind-driven rain felt like needles in my eyes.

"We'll make a turn in a few minutes," Dad shouted. "The island should be behind us by now. Hand me the chart."

Standing at the wheel, trying to keep the *Elizabeth's* bow to the wind, Dad started to unfold the chart, but a quick gust of wind grabbed it.

We all scrambled to catch it, but we were too late.

As the *Elizabeth* surfed up and down the steep waves night descended, and the already dark sky turned pitch black. Without the chart it was impossible to tell if we were still in the deep channel that led to the open sea. Blinking my eyes, I thought I saw a light, but I couldn't be sure.

Suddenly Dad screamed. "Watch out! Hang on!"

As the monster wave lifted us high into the sky, I felt my belly flip over. I was about to be sick, when we came thudding down.

"We're aground," Dad shouted. "Go below. Tell your mother to get the kids dressed. We have a serious situation here."

When I pushed the companionway hatch back, I saw Mom sitting on top of the dinette table. She had one arm around Gale, the other around Tim. Every life jacket in the boat was piled around them. The fancy ring buoy Dad was so proud of --- *Elizabeth*---Chicago--- hug around my mother's neck. She was sobbing. "Didn't anyone hear me calling?"

I was about to say something soothing, when I noticed water on the galley floor. A kitchen towel, some soggy cereal boxes, and a couple tomatoes surged back and forth in three inches of water.

Without even answering, I wheeled around, scrambled on deck, and grabbed Dad's arm. "There's water in the cabin!" I screamed. "It's over the floorboards! We're sinking!"

After ordering Joe to man the big pitcher-pump, Dad sprinted past me. Down below, I could hear him calling on the radio. "Mayday! Mayday! This is the yacht *Elizabeth*. We are hard aground near Dog Island. We're taking on water. Repeat... this is the yacht *Elizabeth*. Mayday...Mayday..."

As Joe worked the long pump handle, a steady stream of water poured over its iron lip. Every time a wave came, it lifted and dropped the *Elizabeth*, burying her keel deeper and deeper into the sandy bottom.

"Without a receiver, we won't even know if anyone heard him," Joe said.

"Well, we're only in five feet of water, so she can't really sink." I said. "As soon as it's light, someone is bound to see us."

When Dad came back on deck, he looked haggard. "If this pounding continues, she'll break up," he said. "Lucky for us, the eye of the storm must have hit farther up the coast. She's opened a few seams, but I think the pump can keep up with it. We should know soon if the Coast Guard heard us. In the meantime let's try to kedge her off. Come on, Joe. Let's get the dinghy in the water. If we drop the anchor in deep water, we might be able to pull ourselves off this sandbar."

When Joe brought the dinghy around, it bucked against the waves and swirled sideways. "Watch your hands," Dad said. "Take her out about fifty feet before you drop the anchor."

As I watched Joe row off into the darkness, I felt sorry for him. The way his oars kept coming out of the water, it was obvious he wasn't experienced. After a few minutes and much circling around, he was only about twenty feet away.

"Put your back into it, boy!" Dad shouted through cupped hands.

"Oh, come on!" I moaned. "Joe doesn't know how to row. You're sending him out into the middle of a hurricane, Dad!"

Dad ignored me. "Put you back into, Joe. Row harder!"

Riding an unexpected lull in the wind, Joe's angry voice bounced back to us.

"Screw you old man!"

"That boy needs to learn some manners." Dad muttered.

After he made sure the anchor was holding, Dad called Joe back aboard. "I'm going to need everyone except Tim on deck." Dad put his hand on my shoulder. "Go get your mother and Gale."

A few minutes later, we all stood behind him in the bow. Like in a game of tug of war, we each grabbed hold of the anchor rode.

"When I give the word," Dad said, "everyone pull."

Mom had a hand on Joe's shoulder. Gale was behind me.

"Okay!" Dad yelled. "Pull!"

With loud groans and strained muscles, we pulled as hard as we could.

"Harder!" Dad commanded. "Harder!"

The urgency in his voice made us double our efforts, but the *Elizabeth* just sat there.

"Forget it, kids." Dad let go of the rope. "It's hopeless. "

Returning to the cockpit, we huddled in silent despair for hours. As the *Elizabeth* nudged deeper into the sandbar with each passing wave, our eyes scanned the horizon in hopes of seeing a Coast Guard boat coming, but only darkness surrounded us. When the sky finally did glow with light, we were amazed to see we were only a few hundred yards off shore.

Dad grabbed his binoculars. "There's a restaurant on the beach. I think it's open," he said. "I see a few cars." But, a few minutes later, Tim yelled, "I see a boat coming."

When the 40-foot cutter got close enough, a coast guardsman wearing an orange life-vest shouted through a megaphone. "Did you call for assistance, Sir?"

"Yes! We're hard aground. We need a tow."

"Stand by. I'll toss you a line."

It took several attempts, but eventually Dad caught the big hawser. After he wrapped it around our bow bitts, two four-inch chunks of solid oak that went all the way down to the *Elizabeth's* iron keel, he waved okay, and the steel cutter revved its motors.

"Everybody hold on! Get ready for her to come off."

Rolling first right, then left, the *Elizabeth* shuddered as she inched forward, but then a cracking sound shot through the air, and the bitts came flying past us.

Holy mackerel!

When they realized what happened, the Coast Guard boat circled back. It tried to come alongside us, but the long rollers left over from the storm rocked her violently.

"We're going to have to stand off." The coast guardsman yelled. "It's too dangerous to get closer. I'll bring another cutter out here. But first, we'll evacuate your wife and kids. They'll have to go in the water, one person at a time, but don't worry. It's only a few feet. I'll throw you a line. Wrap it tight around them."

"Oh, no, Edward!" Mom sobbed. "You know I can't swim."

"You won't have to, Marie. They'll pull you over."

After they reeled Mom in, Dad lowered Gale into the water, then Tim.

As we watched the Coast Guard boat head for land, Dad sighed. "Well, at least they're safe," he said. "If they harness the two boats together that ought to be enough to pull us off."

By the time the Coast Guard boats returned, the wind had ceased. The sea was flat calm and the air was sultry. Backing his stern up to the *Elizabeth,* the coast guardsman passed a thick wire cable to Dad. "Here, run this around your main cabin."

As our rescuers took up their positions---one boat off our port side, the other off our starboard, the roar of the revving engines and the billowing smell of diesel blew past us. Once again, the *Elizabeth* responded by moving a few inches forward. Feeling hopeful, I was watching small plumes of sand rise from the bottom, when she tipped to one side. "STOP! STOP!" Dad screamed. "The cable is gnawing through the wood! You're going to rip the whole cabin off! "

Shutting down his engine, the coast guardsman walked to the stern. When he saw the way the cable had chewed up the cabin, he shook his head. "Her keel is buried too deep in the sand. Your only hope is to get a towboat out here. If it backs right up to you, its motor might be strong enough to blow a channel through that sandbar. If you can't find a towboat, then I suggest you contact a salvage company. You can't just leave your boat here. She's a navigation hazard. You could get a big fine."

As we watched the two Coast Guard boats leave, the wrinkles across Dad's forehead deepened. "A towboat will cost a fortune. I hate to say it kids, but this might be the end of the *Elizabeth*. The longer she sits here, the more those seams will open up. Maybe that restaurant has a phone. Let's row over. I guess it can't hurt. We'll see what they charge."

During the long row to the shore, Joe and I sat on the stern thwart. Dad pulled hard on the oars. His sunburned face tilted toward the sky.

Inside the small café, everyone was talking about the storm. As we headed toward an empty booth, the morning news flashed across a TV screen. The eye of the storm had hit land a little north of us, but hundreds of homes were without power. Trees down. Roads closed. When the camera panned through Carrabelle, we saw a lot of heavily damaged boats. "See? I told you." Dad said. "We did the right thing."

Sitting in a booth by the window, Dad flipped through the Yellow Pages. "Your Mom will be worried sick." He said. "I better call her, too."

When Dad came back, he threw the phone book on the table.

"I knew it. They want a thousand bucks an hour!"

Joe shook his head. "Maybe we should hitch back to Carrabelle, Ed. Maybe some of the fishermen there will know what to do."

Dad frowned. "No. I'm not going back there."

Borrowing a pen from the waitress, Dad wrote a list of things he wanted to take off the boat. "Just the valuables," he said. "Things we can't replace. The ship's clock, the sextant, the radios...not a whole lot to account for a man's life is it?"

Unable to bear his pain, I threw my arm around Dad's shoulder.

A man sitting in the booth in front of us wearing a yellow construction hat overheard us. "Did I hear you say you needed a towboat? My brother-in-law has one."

"I don't have enough money for a tow," Dad said.

"Don't worry about that. Looks like you people could lose your boat. Jim's been a sailor his whole life. He'll probably do it for nothing."

When he came back, the stranger was all smiles. "He's coming right over. It'll take about twenty minutes."

Back aboard the boat, I was helping Dad organize the radio room when I heard Joe shout. "They're here! They're here!"

As soon as the towboat backed his stern close to the *Elizabeth's* bow, greasy blobs of foam swirled past her hull. The water around us boiled and churned. When I felt the *Elizabeth* slowly slide off the sandbar, I felt so relieved; I almost threw up.

"Where do you want to go?" The towboat owner shouted. "I'll give you a tow."

Dad looked warily toward the shore. "Can you take us to the Coast Guard station? My wife and kids are there."

After the boats were tied up, Dad jumped ashore and so did the towboat captain.

"Jim Thorpe." The man said.

"Ed Goodlander." Dad's mouth sagged and went sideways. "No way, I can ever thank you enough."

The man shrugged. "Can't count the number of times people helped me out. Happy to return the favor."

After asking the coast guard commander's permission to stay overnight, Dad brought Mom and the kids back. Mom chewed her bottom lip as she surveyed the damage to the cabin and the mess below. "What's the plan, Edward? Can we make it to St. Pete?"

"If I can slow those leaks, we should be fine. We'll just have to pump a lot."

That night Dad gathered us all in the cockpit.

"I think I have a solution." He grinned. "Toilet wax. Remember that hardware store guy in Cairo? Maybe that'll stop the leaks."

The next day one of the coast guardsmen took us to a big plumbing supply house in Apalachicola.

"Can I help you?"

"Yes, I need some toilet rings."

"How many?"

"All you got."

The next morning, Dad pulled a machine I'd never seen before and a blue Medusa diving mask from under his bunk. Placing them at Joe's feet, he smiled. "Hey, guess what, kiddo? I'm going to let you dive down to plug up the leaks. I wish I had a better mask, but this will work." After duct-taping a hose to one of the holes and sealing the other, Dad assured Joe it would be an easy dive. "Just push the wax into any open seams you find." Dad fastened a weight belt around Joe's waist and tied a rope to it. "If you run into any problems, yank on this. I'll pull you right up."

As I watched the top of Joe's head disappear beneath the water, Dad patted his machine. "I knew this compressor would come in handy someday." He said. "I can't believe the things people throw away."

Joe had only been down a few minutes when one of the Coast Guard guys came looking for Dad. "The captain needs to see you right away." He said. "It's about staying here more than 24 hours."

Dad handed Joe's safety-line over to Tim. "I'll only be gone a minute. You keep an eye on him. If you feel him pull on the rope, you and Carole bring him up fast."

Expecting the repair job to take a while, I decided to go below to get a book. "If anything happens, Tim, call me."

When I came back on deck, Tim had his nose buried in an Archie comic. The safety-line next to him jerked a few times, and then it stopped. Sprinting across the deck, I grabbed the rope and started pulling. Tim got behind me "I'm sorry," he said. "Just pull." I growled.

When we finally got Joe back aboard the boat, he ripped the Medusa mask off his face. Weaving around the deck, he ground his knuckles into his eyes. "Jesus Christ! I was pulling on the rope. Where were you guys!" Joe rolled his lips back to expose his teeth. "Can you see any flecks? That damn compressor had paint in it! I was eating that shit! Were the hell is Ed?"

"The captain wanted to see him," I said.

"Well, the next time he needs a diver, tell him no thanks. I'm nobody's frigging guinea pig."

When Dad returned, he was smiling. "Good news. We can stay one more day. How'd it go Joe? Get those leaks fixed?

Joe held up the Medusa mask with its paint-freckled faceplate. His eyes darted toward the water and back.

"Holy cow! Dad put his hands on his hips. "Someone must have used it as a paint compressor."

Tim put his hand on Joe's leg. "He was dizzy when he came up."

"Gee, I'm really sorry, son."

When Joe heard the word *son*, his face softened, and my heart skipped a beat. It was the first time he'd been anointed with that word, and Joe beamed. "That's okay, Ed. I got the leaks fixed. There were only two seams. It took a while for those fumes to build up."

On our trip to St. Pete, in spite of the repairs, we had to pump every three hours to keep the water from seeping over the *Elizabeth's* floorboards, but our spirits were high. Freed once again from the shore, we slipped right back into our daily routine. One sunny afternoon, Joe and I were sitting alone on the foredeck. Above our head, cumulous lambs danced across a blue sky. When I leaned back against him, I let out a sigh.

"Are you okay?" he asked.

"Sure, I'm just a little tired. I'm happy really."

"Me, too," he said. "Happier than I've ever been."

"Only sometimes I feel scared something will happen. I'm afraid I'll lose you."

"Not a chance!" Joe laughed. "I love you. I'll love you forever."

"Forever?" I grinned.

"Forever and ever, Carole. And, I really mean it."

The cozy dock Dad found in St. Pete was every yachtsman's dream. With its white picket gate, electricity and water, it even had a public telephone mounted on a pole at the end. Directly across the street from us, the pink Vinoy Hotel with its stately palm trees sprawled across a green lawn.

"It'll be our front yard," Mom said.

A few weeks after we arrived, Dad got a job managing a sign shop, and he hired Joe to help him. I went right to Walgreen's.

The people who lived along the docks by the hotel called them *Paradise Docks*, and they really were a yachtsman's heaven. Every night all the boat people gathered to cook up a community feast. None of them had any money, but they all had a story to tell. Wine flowed and laughter spilled across the water. When Dad played his guitar, everyone sang,

The *Elizabeth* was still leaking, so we had to keep checking the bilge. A small faceplate on the galley floor made it possible to see how high the water was, so Dad was always peering into it with a worried look on his face. We called it his "psycho-hole".

It was obvious to anyone who knew anything about boats that the wrenched keel meant the *Elizabeth* could never be made seaworthy again, but Dad refused to accept that notion. Every day some new repair scheme bubbled up. "Maybe I'll put a cement coating over her whole hull or sheath the bottom in copper." Someone suggested fiberglass, a new medium that people were using to build boats, but all those things cost money, a lot of money, and Dad didn't have any.

One night Joe and I were at a party aboard a big Trumpy yacht that had just come up from Key West. Sitting on a plush sofa in the pilot house, Joe said, "Let's get married. I mean soon. Like next week. I've been thinking about our future. Florida's great, but the wages here stink. Your dad is never going to get the boat fixed. Maybe we should go north. They have a sign-painting school in Boston. I could commute from Taunton. "

"A sign-painting school? Dad never went to school. He got an apprenticeship."

"Well, I looked it up in the library." Joe grinned. "It's called Butera School of Art. The have night classes. I'll get a day job, of course, maybe hanging signs. I'm doing that now with your dad."

The idea of moving so far away scared me, but if Joe was going to be my husband, wasn't it my job to support him? Wasn't that what good wives did?

"We don't even have a car, Joe."

"No problem. I got a side-job yesterday painting the wall around Ray's Motel. He said he'd give us a free room until the job is done. Between my salary and yours, we'll be able save enough to rent an apartment, then in a few months a car."

"But, what if he finds a way to fix the boat? It wouldn't surprise me. My dad can do anything."

"That would take a miracle, Carole. He'd have to put a new keel on her, and that's impossible. You're a grown woman. Soon we'll have a family of our own. Your parents will figure something out. I want to buy us a house someday. I want to take care of our baby. In order to do that I need a trade, like your Dad. He can find work anywhere."

As Joe laid out his plan for our life, I thought about Mom, how much she had always wanted a house.

"So what do you say? You want to go?"

"Sure, if that's what you think is best, Joe...but I don't want to tell my parents about the baby yet. There's plenty of time. After we're up north, I'll let write then."

When we got back to the *Elizabeth,* Dad was sitting with his back against the cabin. Mom had her head in his lap. "As soon she's seaworthy again," Dad was saying. "We'll head for Key West. It's only 90 miles from there to Cuba. The Spanish used to own it. Narrow streets. Old forts. Pineapple plantations. You're going to love the history there."

Joe and I sat down on the cabin-top. I felt anxious, but Joe dove right in.

"Carole and I decided we should get married. Next week, probably. As soon as we can save enough, we're going to buy a car and head north. I found a sign-painting school in Boston. I need some kind of skill."

"You mean move ashore?" Dad grimaced. "You don't have to do that, Joe. Once you're married, I'll let you sleep together. You can have the fo'scle. Tim can sleep in the dinette and Gale can sleep on the sofa. "

Mom put her hand on Dad's chest. "Don't be silly, Edward. The kids want a place of their own."

On a bright sunny day in August, Joe and I were married by a Justice of the Peace. I wore a white suit I found at the Dollar Store. Joe wore black chinos and a white shirt. It was a brief ceremony. The friendly old man just said a few words and suddenly we were man and wife. It was an exhilarating feeling. I felt grown up and ready for a new life.

On the courthouse steps, Tim and Gale gave us their wedding presents-two washcloths and a dishtowel. Mom said her and Dad were going to take us dinner, to a five-star restaurant in Ybor City. It was called the Columbia. She'd found it in *Holiday* magazine. That was their present. Dad said he'd paid a friend of Gale's to take us there. Because he couldn't afford to take

everyone to the restaurant, Gale and Tim and the friend were
going to eat at McDonalds. Afterwards, they'd explore the town;
then pick us up in a couple of hours.

With its strolling violinists, interior fountains, and Old
World décor, the Columbia Restaurant was charming. Mom had
to sample everything, so she kept ordering all kinds of delicious
side dishes and the desserts sitting on a little tray they wheeled to
the table made everyone's eyes pop.

"I bet Cuba is just like this," Mom said.

When it came time to pay the bill, Dad called the waiter
over. "What's this?" He held up the check. "I told you not to let
me go over fifty dollars."

The waiter just looked at him.

"Well, of course, I thought you were joking."

"Well, I wasn't," Dad said. "That's all the money I have."

The waiter looked confused. "I don't know what to say. I'm
sure the manager will let you go home and get it."

"Get what? There's no money at home. Fifty bucks is all I
have. "

Mom looked nervous. "This is our daughter's wedding
night," she said.

At first I was shocked, then embarrassed. I could feel heat in my face, but then I realized this was classic, this was my family, and in an odd sort of way that made me happy,

Giving me a sympathetic look, the waiter softened. "Congratulations", he said. "How unfortunate!" There was an awkward pause, but then his eyes twinkled. "My wedding present," he said. "I'll pay the rest of the bill myself."

When we stood up to leave, Joe assured him we'd pay him back as soon as we were settled in Massachusetts---maybe not all at once, but eventually. So Juan Carlos wrote his name on a postcard he grabbed at the front desk.

"Be sure to add a nice tip for yourself," Mom said.

The efficiency apartment Joe and I rented had palm trees in the yard, jalousie windows, and a terrazzo floor. The kitchen wasn't much bigger than the boat's main cabin, but it had a big bedroom, and a small cement pad with a picnic table outside.

The first time Tim visited, he raced from room to room admiring all my abundant conveniences. Turning the kitchen-sink faucets off and on, he giggled when a powerful stream of hot water gurgling through his cupped hands. When he came to our gleaming white Westinghouse gas stove, he examined the row of red knobs on the top. Turning one on, he leaped backwards when the circle of blue flames shot in the air. "Hey, you don't even need a match!" With the enthusiasm of an aborigine plucked down in the middle of New York City, he picked p the phone. I didn't know anyone to call, so I dialed up the weather lady and Joe and I bent in half laughing, as we listened to Tim's one-sided conversation.

"Gee," Tim said. "You guys are living high off the hog."

Letting Tim explore the apartment alone, Joe grabbed a newspaper to look for car ads while I started dinner. When the spaghetti was almost done, I called Tim, but he didn't answer.

"Go find him," I said.

A few minutes later, Joe returned with a big smile on his face. "Come look at this, Carole."

Tim had fallen asleep in the shower. Curled up at the bottom of the small stall, his body was in, but his head resting on a limp arm was out. Soft as a summer rain the water from the shower head sprayed over him.

"God, I am really going to miss this little guy," Joe said.

"Me, too! My whole family."

Joe nudged me with his elbow. "Even Gale?"

"Especially, Gale, I love my little sister."

Dad only visited our apartment once. When I suggested he might like to take a shower, he declined. "Too much hot water isn't good for you," he said. "I don't want to mess up my body's natural balance."

Mom, on the other hand, came by often. She enjoyed sitting outside reading magazines at the picnic table or cooking a special dinner. One night she brought her "house chest" over, a cardboard box full of treasures she'd lovingly collected for the house she hoped Dad would someday buy her. Watching my mother carefully unwrap her china tea cups, fancy porcelain vases and gold rimmed dessert plates, I felt like hugging her. I knew her chances of ever owning a house were slim. I knew Dad would never give up trying to fix the boat. For him, moving ashore was not just a terrible thought. It spelled utter defeat.

Holding up a red and gold Japanese fan, Mom smiled. "Just look at this, Carole!"

"Oh, that's beautiful, Mom. It'll go good with your gong, if you ever get one."

When she pulled out a long, gold cigarette holder and stuck it between her teeth, I had to laugh.

"So what do you think of this?"

"But, you don't even smoke!"

Mom looked insulted. "Well, I could take it up you know."

The 1940 black Desoto Joe bought was battered and dented, but it was a bargain. "This thing is built like a tank." He bragged. "The engine's so clean you could eat off it."

The day before we left St. Petersburg, I quit my job. Even though I hadn't been there very long, the waitresses gave me a going-away party. That night, balloons decorated our apartment. When I hung their "Good Luck" banner over our bed, I felt truly grateful for all the good wishes that would follow us north.

The morning of our departure, Joe and I piled our belongings into the trunk. We only had our clothes and two milk crates full of personal items. My entire wardrobe at that time consisted of three bathing suits, one cotton dress, a couple of pairs of shorts and some T-shirts. One of the girls at work had given me a full-length fake-fur Borgana coat.

"You'll need this. It'll be cold up there. It was my mother's favorite when she lived in New Jersey. I never wear it."

Realizing the reality of the moment, I had mixed feelings. It was heart wrenching to leave my family, but my head was also full of visions about the future---Joe and I driving north, him having a trade, our baby.

When we went down to the boat to say our final goodbyes, Joe and Dad shook hands, and Mom started crying. Gale said she was going to miss me, so I told her she could come north anytime she wanted to, maybe stay a whole summer. Walking back to the car, Tim grabbed my hand. "Be careful you don't let the Dreamchrushers get you," he said. "They love to live on land."

That made me laugh.

As we drove away from the harbor, as Joe shifted into low gear and turned the corner leading to the highway, I could already feel myself shedding the past. Like the *wahines* in Tahiti, I had learned to say goodbye. Like ships we come and go, but there is always another port, another wonderful adventure waiting beyond the horizon.

Moving closer to Joe, I put my hand on his chest. "I love you, Joe."

"I love you, too."

When I think about our trip now and Dad's dream, I know some people might think the whole thing was a failure, but I don't see it that way. One of my favorite poems is *Ithaka* by Constantine P. Kadafy. In it, he says,

When you set out on your journey to Ithaca,
pray that the road is long,
full of adventure, full of knowledge.
The Lestrygonians and the Cyclops,
the angry Poseidon -- do not fear them:
You will never find such as these on your path,
if your thoughts remain lofty, if a fine
emotion touches your spirit and your body"

Well, our journey had certainly been long. The dream of Tahiti nourished us. It propelled us forward, but it was really the day-to-day living that was so rewarding, so important. At the end of his poem, Kadafy says:

Ithaca has given you the beautiful voyage.
Without her you would have never set out on the road.
She has nothing more to give you.
And if you find her poor, Ithaca has not deceived you.
Wise as you have become, with so much experience,
you must already have understood what Ithacas mean.

Dreamseekers know things that other people don't know. They know that life is full of surprises, like the river it's full of twists and turns. There is deep water, then there are shoals, but to them there is no such thing as failure because they live in the moment. When they have a hunger for something, they go for it.

They take risks. Like steering by the North Star when out of sight of land, they have faith they will arrive at the right destination.

The last time I saw my father, he was in a nursing home. We'd tried to take care of him, but Parkinson's had ravaged his body to the point where he needed around the clock nursing care. The day he was admitted, his eyes signaled his sense of betrayal. "I should have opened up the sea cocks, headed for open water and gone down with the ship. This place looks like a prison."

When I brought him his lunch on a thin metal tray the last day I visited him, I couldn't help but notice how much happier he looked. "There's a big storm brewing, Carole." An odd grin had spread across his face. "Better get those sails down."

Gulping hard, I raised my hand to my eyebrow and gave him a sharp salute.

"Aye, aye, captain," I said. "But, don't worry. Our ship is built for this kind of weather."

As I walked toward the nursing home parking lot, I looked up at the sky. Small wispy mare's tails rode a high wind. Suddenly, a great feeling of comfort came over me. I knew Dad's spirit was already sailing up there. Freed from all ailments, with the wind at his back, he was headed downwind toward the endless horizon.

Never at home on the land.

Epilogue

GALE NEVER WAVERED IN her interest in Native Americans.
The summer camp Blacksnake (her Native American name)
established and currently runs with her painter husband in New
England, teaches ecology and Native American lore. It is
legendary for its creative curriculum. My sister was the first one
to graduate from college. She is a certified Reiki practitioner who
has studied with Buddhist monks. Gale married three times. She
has three children and a tribe of gifted grandchildren.

Timmy grew up to be a world famous sailor. He bought the *Corrina*, his first boat, when he was only sixteen years old. Then he paired up with Carolyn his high school sweetheart and never lived ashore again. Their daughter Roma never lived in a house. She was raised in the Virgin Islands aboard the *Carlotta* Tim's second boat.

Recently Timmy (now known in boating circles as Captain Fatty Goodlander) and Carolyn completed their second circumnavigation of the world aboard *Wild Card*, his last boat. The monthly articles he writes for *Cruising World* magazine and his five published books have gained him droves of enchanted fans from all over the world. Wherever I go, people are always saying, "**You're** Captain Fatty's sister!" Oh, how proud Dad would have been of his first born son.

My youngest brother, Morgan, founder of the Gestalt Institute of San Francisco, never sailed aboard the *Elizabeth*, but he did, before Dad got sick, take another trip down the Mississippi River with him. Morgan lives in San Francisco now, and Mom lives in Santa Cruz. The two of them enjoy sailing around the Bay or riding on his motorcycle. At 93, in spite of being legally blind, Mom hasn't slowed down much. She likes it when we call her the Sea Siren, and she loves to regale the people

in her apartment building with salty stories of life aboard the
Elizabeth.

During our eighteen years together, Joe and I lived a
nomadic life full of romance and adventure. We traveled across
this country and Mexico many times, built two boats, lived on a
commune, and raised four beautiful children, Gary, Angie,
Cindy, and Josh. Our marriage didn't last, but our love did. Even
though we divorced and married other people, and then divorced
them, when Joe was killed in a motorcycle accident in 1990, I felt
like a bereaved widow. A few weeks before he died, he stopped by
my house to give me a gift. He didn't stay long, so I didn't open it
until after he was gone. It was a Leonard Cohen tape, and that
was very surprising. During the time we were married, I played
Cohen's songs over and over, but Joe was definitely not a Leonard
Cohen fan. When I read the title of the tape, *I'm Your Man*, tears
filled my eyes. Yes, he was, and yes, he always would be—forever
and ever.

Carole Ann Borges was born on the south-side of Chicago. She spent most of her childhood traveling to that spot just beyond the horizon. Borges is a widely published writer. Her poems and essays have appeared in *Poetry, Kalliope, Crosscurrents,* and numerous other literary magazines. As a freelance journalist, she has been featured in *Dorchester Community News* in Boston, *West Side Gazette* and *Downtown Hollywood* newspapers in Ft. Lauderdale, and *The Enlightener* newspaper in Knoxville. Twice she was nominated for a Pushcart Prize and in 1987 was the recipient of an award by the Massachusetts Artist's Foundation. Borges currently lives in Knoxville, Tennessee, with her two dogs, Karma and Krishna, and Mr. Dunwoody, a handsome cat.

26801627R00192

Made in the USA
Charleston, SC
19 February 2014